60 Essential Recipes
to Take You From
AMATEUR TO PRO

TEEN BAKING

BOOTCAMP

MATTHEW MERRIL

Finalist on Food Network's *Kids Baking Championship*

PAGE STREET
PUBLISHING CO.

First published in 2021 by
Page Street Publishing Co.
27 Congress Street, Suite 105
Salem, MA 01970
www.pagestreetpublishing.com

Distributed by Macmillan, sales in Canada by The Canadian Manda Group.

25 24 23 22 21   1 2 3 4 5

ISBN-13: 978-1-64567-464-1
ISBN-10: 1-64567-464-9

Library of Congress Control Number: 2021931965

Cover and book design by Meg Baskis for Page Street Publishing Co.
Photography by Thomas McGovern

Printed and bound in the United States

TO MY MOM.

I owe any success I have in both
the culinary world and in life to her.

CONTENTS

INTRODUCTION

Hello, bakers, and welcome to *Teen Baking Bootcamp*. My name is Matthew and I'm your chef guide who'll take you from home baker to pastry pro. Ever since I was a kid (even though I'm currently 16 . . .), I've always been fascinated by baking—but I wasn't always good at it. From ages 8 to 10, I learned everything I knew about baking by watching YouTube videos and Food Network. From then on, I went from whipping up batches of cookies in my kitchen to crafting cupcakes on national television after scoring the chance of a lifetime to be on Food Network's *Kids Baking Championship*. Fueled by my 10-year-old self's passion for desserts, I dragged my reluctant mom to Hollywood for 3 weeks, marking the beginning of a cooking career I am so grateful to pursue. Following my placement as a finalist in the eight-episode installment, I appeared in several other food competitions, such as *Holiday Baking Championship*, *Chopped Junior* and *Guy's Grocery Games*. Between these appearances, I worked with Avocados from Mexico as a brand ambassador, performing live demos across the country.

Following my work on Food Network, I went on a brief hiatus during my first year of high school to refine my culinary skills. My big return to the media-cooking world took place when I started my TikTok page, @MatthewInTheKitchen. The unexpected success after creating a few cooking videos about my time on *Kids Baking Championship* evolved into a full-fledged job, bringing me opportunities I could never have fathomed. Working with brands like Pillsbury, writing my own cookbook (whaaaat??) and having an audience of more than 2 million people are aspects of this culinary endeavor I am grateful for every day. At the core of these cooking ventures, there's a wide-eyed 10-year-old, so eager to learn everything he could about culinary arts. There was something so satisfying about being self-taught with no assistance, which inspired me to write a cookbook—a manual for people like me, a place where every technique I needed could be found.

Each recipe is equipped with a measure of its difficulty, from one whisk to three whisks. One whisk signifies the recipe is designed for budding bakers. A recipe with two whisks is for bakers looking to broaden their horizons, yet without certain intricacies and techniques that pose a big challenge. Three-whisk recipes are for bold bakers who aren't afraid of any culinary test. A recipe with three whisks uses advanced techniques, but produces an end product worthy of the difficulty. The goal is to cultivate your skills to make you a better baker. Each recipe provides its own set of challenges (some more than others), but I believe with the right dedication, you can make each and every recipe in this book. While writing the recipes, I was determined to explain various pitfalls I encountered when making some of these dishes. I hope the clarity of each recipe will help guide you along your baking journey.

You may be wondering why the title of this cookbook is *Teen Baking Bootcamp*. The name implies that this book is for teenagers to work on their skills in the kitchen. But, there is, in fact, a double meaning. The title *Teen Baking Bootcamp* also refers to the fact that I am a teen, giving you the fundamental baking knowledge required for each recipe in a way that is clear for all readers. Thus, this cookbook isn't just for teens. Aspiring bakers of any age can look to the recipes for guidance on possible errors in recipes and gaining basic culinary skills to avoid any kitchen conundrums.

Last, I want to say thank you for taking this journey with me. Whether you've been following me since my days on Food Network, found me through my social media accounts or if this is our first time meeting, I am so honored to be able to share my passion with you. Follow along and soon you'll be the best baker on the block.

MATTHEW'S KiTCHEN RUNDOWN

Before we get started, let's review a few tips and tricks that will help you along the way.

iMPORTANT TERMS

+ **Blind-bake/par-bake:** This technique is when you bake a pie crust before adding a filling that does not need to be baked (blind-bake) or when you slightly bake (par-bake) a crust before adding a filling that *does* get baked to ensure the crust doesn't become soggy.

+ **Dock:** Docking refers to poking a bunch of holes into unbaked pie dough in a baking dish, generally when blind-baking a crust, to allow even airflow to create a delicious crust.

+ **Fold:** Folding is one of the most important techniques in all of baking. When making a dessert that requires whipped egg whites to be stirred into a mixture, most of the time you will fold them in. This means very gently stirring, being sure not to deflate the egg whites, which are full of air. Bring a rubber spatula to the bottom of the bowl, scoop the bottom of the mixture to the top in a circular motion and repeat.

+ **Garnish:** A garnish is simply something to decorate your dish with, generally edible.

+ **Preheat:** Always turn your oven on before you prepare your dishes so your baked goods cook evenly!

+ **Proof:** Proofing dough is the process of letting it rise. Place your dough in a large, greased bowl, cover with a kitchen towel, then allow it to sit in a warm area for as long as the recipe specifies.

+ **Stiff/medium peaks:** When whipping a meringue, the way to know it is done is if it reaches "stiff peaks" (or some other variant of peak firmness depending on the recipe).

+ **Temper:** When making desserts like custard, with eggs used to thicken the custard base, tempering is the process of slightly heating up the eggs so that they don't scramble when added to the hot milk. This technique involves adding half of the hot milk mixture into the egg/egg yolk mixture, stirring, then pouring the newly warmed yolks back into the pot of milk.

+ **Zest:** Use a grater to shred bits of citrus peel (generally lemons, limes or oranges). The oil of the fruit is stored in the rind, giving your desserts a great flavor. Be careful because you don't want to get any of the white pith into the shreds, as this part of the fruit is super bitter.

HELPFUL HiNTS

+ **Allow your cakes to cool** completely before frosting them! I sometimes wrap mine in plastic and refrigerate them overnight just to ensure the frosting doesn't melt.

+ **To release cakes from their pans,** first make sure you have thoroughly greased and floured your pan (see more detail in the recipes), then run a knife or spatula around the edge, and finally invert the pan onto a cooling rack or plate.

+ **To measure dry ingredients properly,** spoon them into the measuring cup as opposed to scooping with the measuring cup. This step prevents you from adding too much of one ingredient.

+ **When making yeasted dough,** don't skimp on the kneading! I used to make this mistake all the time growing up, and achieving a smooth dough really makes a difference.

+ **To frost a cake,** spread a generous amount (1 to 2 cups [270 to 540 g]) of frosting on the bottom layer of the cake, then add the top layer. Place half of the remaining frosting on top of the cake and use a spatula to spread the frosting very thinly all over the top and the sides of the cake. Chill the cake for 30 minutes, then smooth the remainder of the frosting all over the sides and top of the cake.

+ **Whenever you decorate cakes,** I always recommend leveling the cakes, meaning cutting off the rounded edge on top of the cake. This will make your cakes easier to frost. I use a serrated knife, but this process can be tricky. If you aren't up for leveling cakes, make sure you flip the top layer of cake upside down when decorating, so the top of the cake is flat instead of dome shaped.

+ **When separating the yolks from the whites,** you will notice the egg yolk is an enclosed sphere, but it can pop. If your egg yolk pops into the egg white, the frosting will not work. Have no fear because I have designed the perfect process for any beginners who are intimidated by this step. Take out three bowls. Crack an egg into the first bowl, and using your hands (it will be slimy!), scoop out the egg yolk. Place the yolk into the second bowl then pour the egg white into the third bowl. Repeat this step with each egg, and if an egg yolk breaks, you can simply discard the egg (or save it to scramble!).

+ Two ingredients I frequently use but rarely have on hand are buttermilk and cake flour. Both of these can be created using pantry staples.

    + **Cake flour:** To make 1 cup (120 g) of cake flour, place 1 cup (125 g) of all-purpose flour into a bowl, then remove 2 tablespoons (16 g). Add 2 tablespoons (16 g) of cornstarch and stir.

    + **Buttermilk:** To make 1 cup (240 ml) of buttermilk, mix 1 cup (240 ml) of regular milk with 1 tablespoon (15 ml) of lemon juice or white vinegar and let it sit for 5 minutes. It is OK if it becomes lumpy.

+ **When using a stand mixer,** there are multiple attachments or "stirrer-thingies" that you can use. The paddle attachment that looks like, well, a ping-pong paddle, is perfect for creaming together butter and sugar in a cookie or cake recipe. Essentially, this beats together ingredients and is the standard stirrer. Then you have the whisk attachment. The whisk attachment is used for . . . anything that would require a whisk by hand. Generally, we always whip egg whites into a meringue using the whisk attachment. It is also great for aerating ingredients. I use a whisk attachment when making frosting because of the light texture it gives buttercream. The last attachment is called a dough hook, which you would put on your mixer to knead dough instead of breaking a sweat kneading dough for 20 minutes.

MY FAVORITE TOOLS

+ **Silicone mat:** Instead of using parchment paper on cookie sheets, silicone mats are the literal best alternative. They are perfect for every type of cookie or anything you could possibly bake on a cookie sheet (plus they are reusable!).

+ **Offset spatula:** This spatula is perfect for cake decorating!!

+ **Ice-cream scoop:** I use a small-sized ice-cream scoop to measure out even portions of cookies onto a tray and even to portion off cupcake batter.

+ **Piping bags:** The ziptop-bag technique only works for so long when you need to control the amount of dough or frosting that you are using! Purchasing piping bags really takes you up a few notches as a baker.

+ **Rotating cake stand:** A cake turntable is crucial if you want the edges of your cake to be perfectly smooth. Holding an offset spatula parallel to the cake and gently rotating the turntable is the preferred method for frosting a cake.

ALL-STAR CAKES

Cakes are honestly a perfect dessert. It has taken me many years to experiment with various cake and frosting combinations, but discovering how different flavors meld together and trying new decoration techniques brought me to love the art of cake making. Growing up, I struggled to find cake recipes that were any good. Most notably, in the finale of Food Network's *Kids Baking Championship*, I whipped up a chocolate cake that, to both mine and the judges' dismay, lacked chocolate flavor!! Eleven-year-old me was inspired to look for and test new recipes that I knew I could rely on. Here are my all-star cakes.

CLASSIC VANILLA CAKE WITH CHOCOLATE BUTTERCREAM

YIELD: One 8-inch (20-cm) two-layer cake

DIFFICULTY: 🥄

Nothing screams "celebration!" quite like vanilla cake paired with chocolate buttercream. I dream about this food combo. The delicious flavor of the cake mixed with the rich cocoa frosting creates a bite that is equally nostalgic and exciting. This recipe is just everything you could possibly want in a cake! You'd better keep this cake recipe in your back pocket because although it is simple to make, it will delight *all* guests!

VANILLA CAKE

Cooking spray

3 cups (375 g) all-purpose flour, plus more for the pans

1 tbsp (14 g) baking powder

¼ tsp salt

½ cup (114 g; 1 stick) unsalted butter, at room temperature

½ cup (120 ml) vegetable oil (see Notes)

1½ cups (300 g) granulated sugar

1 tbsp (15 ml) vanilla extract

4 eggs

1¼ cups (300 ml) buttermilk (see Notes)

Preheat the oven to 350°F (175°C). You will need two 8-inch (20-cm) cake pans. Spray the pans thoroughly with cooking spray or brush with butter. Be sure to coat the edges to prevent sticking. Sprinkle a few tablespoons of flour into each pan, covering the edges with flour by rotating the pans. Discard any flour that does not stick. Preparing your cake pans this way will avoid any kitchen catastrophes!

Pour the flour, baking powder and salt into a large bowl and stir together.

Place the butter, vegetable oil and sugar together in a large bowl. Using a stand mixer, hand mixer or a wooden spoon, beat the ingredients together until they turn pale and fluffy, around 3 minutes.

Pour in the vanilla, and stir in the eggs one at a time. Make sure each egg is fully incorporated before adding the next!

To complete the batter, add the flour mixture and buttermilk in a pattern of dry-wet-dry. In other words, add some of the flour mixture, then some of the buttermilk, and so on until you run out of ingredients to add. I learned when I was an aspiring baker to start by adding the dry ingredients and finish by adding the dry ingredients. This small step will prevent your batter from separating.

Evenly spread the batter in the cake pans and bake for 30 to 35 minutes, or until you can insert a toothpick into the cake and it comes out clean.

(continued)

CHOCOLATE BUTTERCREAM

1 cup (227 g; 2 sticks) butter, at room temperature

2 cups (240 g) powdered sugar

¾ cup (66 g) cocoa powder

¼ tsp salt

2 tbsp (30 ml) evaporated milk (see Notes)

Fruit and chocolate shavings, for garnish (optional)

To make the frosting, add the butter to a large bowl. If using a stand mixer, I recommend using the whisk attachment. Mix the butter on high speed until it turns pale, and then slowly add the powdered sugar. Be sure not to whisk too fast or the powdered sugar will fly everywhere (I learned that lesson the hard way!). Stir in the cocoa powder and salt, then the evaporated milk. Once incorporated, you will have a beautiful, fluffy batch of chocolate frosting.

To assemble, first cool the cakes by flipping the pans onto a cooling rack or plate. Allow the cakes to cool for at least 1 hour, until the cake is room temperature. If the cakes are even slightly warm, the frosting will melt all over the cake and you will be left with a mess!

Place a generous layer of frosting (one-quarter to one-third of the frosting) on top of one cake, then smooth it out into an even layer. Add the top layer of cake. Place about one third of the remaining frosting on top of the cake and use a spatula to spread this layer thinly around the entire cake. This layer of frosting is called a "crumb coat" because it locks in all the crumbs from around the cake. Add the rest of the frosting. My favorite way to decorate is with a rustic, textured look. I achieve this by creating a smooth layer of frosting, then tapping different areas of the cake to create little peaks.

Garnish with fruit and chocolate shavings if you'd like.

NOTES:

Any neutral-flavored oil will work, whether it be vegetable, canola, safflower, peanut and so on.

If you don't have buttermilk, see page 11 to make your own.

If you don't have evaporated milk, you can use regular milk.

THE ONLY CHOCOLATE CAKE YOU'LL EVER NEED WITH SWISS MERINGUE BUTTERCREAM

YIELD: One 9-inch (23-cm) two-layer cake

DIFFICULTY: ✐ ✐ ✐

The challenge of this recipe does not come from the cake, which is a simple, yet tasty, recipe. It is the Swiss meringue buttercream that requires techniques that are pretty advanced. Though the technique is a bit tricky, with some coaching you'll be on your way to the most luxurious buttercream. I have tons of memories of 9-year-old Matthew being so confused about making this seemingly impossible frosting. But I promise, with the right instruction, you *can* make this frosting and oh my goodness it is worth the effort. This frosting is unlike any other buttercream you will ever try, and by far my favorite. It almost tastes like marshmallow! Paired with a decadent chocolate cake, this dessert is simply magic. Don't be alarmed by the egg whites in the recipe! They will be heated to the point where all bacteria are killed.

CHOCOLATE CAKE

Cooking spray

2 cups (250 g) flour, plus more for the pans

2 cups (400 g) sugar

⅔ cup (30 g) cocoa powder

2 tsp (9 g) baking powder

1½ tsp (7 g) baking soda

1 tsp salt

1 tsp instant espresso powder (optional; see Note)

1 cup (240 ml) buttermilk or milk

2 eggs

1 tsp vanilla extract

½ cup (120 ml) vegetable oil

1 cup (240 ml) water

To make the cake, preheat the oven to 350°F (175°C) and prepare two 9-inch (23-cm) cake pans by spraying them with cooking spray or brushing them with melted butter. Be sure to coat the edges to prevent sticking. Sprinkle a few tablespoons of flour into each pan, covering the edges with flour by rotating the pans. Discard any flour that does not stick. Preparing your cake pans this way will avoid any kitchen catastrophes!

Next, add the flour, sugar, cocoa powder, baking powder, baking soda, salt and espresso powder (if using) to a bowl. Whisk together so the ingredients are evenly distributed. Set aside.

In another bowl, combine the buttermilk, eggs, vanilla and oil.

Pour the buttermilk mixture over the dry ingredients and stir together. Be sure to stop stirring right after all of the dry ingredients are absorbed into the liquid! If you mix the batter too much, your cake may be overly chewy!

After you've mixed the dry and wet ingredients, boil the water. When the water is bubbling, remove it from the heat and immediately incorporate it into the batter. Be very careful when mixing because the hot water may splash if you mix too vigorously!

(continued)

SWiSS MERiNGUE BUTTERCREAM

7 egg whites (see egg-separating tips on page 10)

2 cups (400 g) granulated sugar

1½ cups (341 g; 3 sticks) butter, cut into pieces

1 tbsp (15 ml) vanilla extract

¼ tsp salt

NOTE: Instant espresso powder is not required, but it works as a flavor enhancer, making the cake even more chocolate-y and delicious.

Pour your batter evenly between the two prepared cake pans and bake for 30 to 35 minutes, or until you can stick a toothpick into the cake and there is only slight residue on the pick.

To make the frosting, place the egg whites into the bowl of a stand mixer or a large metal bowl if using a hand mixer. Stir in the sugar.

Fill a pot with about 2 inches (5 cm) of water and place the pot on the stove. Bring the water to a boil. Put the bowl with the egg whites on top of the pot of boiling water. Make sure the bowl does not touch the water in the pot below. This is called creating a "double-boiler." The steam from the water in the pot below will heat the egg white mixture without scrambling them. Whisk the egg whites constantly. When the sugar has dissolved, the mixture should read 160°F (70°C) on a candy thermometer. If you don't have a candy thermometer, gather some of the egg white mixture in a spoon and rub it between your fingers. If you can feel sugar granules, you need to continue the heating process (be careful because the mixture will be hot to the touch).

After the sugar has dissolved, place the bowl back into the stand mixer and whisk on high until the egg whites are fully cooled down and have formed what is known as "meringue." The eggs need to be completely cool because if you add the butter to hot meringue, the butter will melt into the meringue and you will end up with a soupy mess. It will take about 15 minutes for the egg whites to cool. When the meringue is cool, gradually add the butter, piece by piece, vanilla and salt. If your meringue is too hot and the butter melts, don't panic! Been there, done that! Place the bowl of sad, melted frosting in the fridge for a few hours then whip again; the butter should solidify and whip up into a beautiful frosting.

The last step is to frost your cake with your new favorite buttercream. Top one layer of the cake with one-quarter of the frosting, and use a spatula to create an even layer of frosting. Top with the second layer of cake, and spread a thin layer of frosting around the entire cake, creating a crumb coat, which locks in the crumbs on the sides of the cake so we get a cleaner finish. Chill the cake for at least 30 minutes, then add the rest of the frosting. I always add the frosting to the top of the cake and spread it from the center, then down the sides of the cake. Then, I hold an offset spatula or flat spatula parallel to the cake and spin the cake, creating smooth edges.

Voilà. Simple, delicious chocolate cake.

EVERYONE'S FAVORITE RED VELVET CAKE WITH CREAM CHEESE FROSTING

YiELD: One 9-inch (23-cm) two-layer cake

DiFFICULTY: 🥄

Red velvet cake is one of the most underrated flavors out there. The light texture of the cake mixed with the tangy cream cheese buttercream is sure to have people coming back for seconds. I brought this cake to a friend for a Halloween celebration and he was talking about how much he loved it for months! A common misconception about red velvet cake is that its flavor is just chocolate dyed red. The cocoa in the cake is not actually for flavor, but provides the cake with the soft texture, which is why it is known as a "velvet" cake.

RED VELVET CAKE

Cooking spray

2⅔ cups (320 g) cake flour (see Notes), plus more for the pans

4 tbsp (22 g) unsweetened cocoa powder

1 tsp baking soda

¼ tsp salt

½ cup (114 g; 1 stick) butter, at room temperature

1¾ cups (350 g) sugar

2 eggs

½ cup (120 ml) vegetable oil, or any neutral-flavored oil

2½ tsp (12 ml) vanilla extract

1 tsp white vinegar

2 tbsp (30 ml) red food coloring

1⅓ cups (320 ml) buttermilk (see Notes)

Preheat the oven to 325°F (165°C) and prepare two 9-inch (23-cm) cake pans. Spray the pans thoroughly with cooking spray or brush with butter. Be sure to coat the edges to prevent sticking. Sprinkle a few tablespoons of flour into each pan, covering the edges with flour by rotating the pans. Discard any flour that does not stick. Preparing your cake pans this way will avoid any kitchen catastrophes!

In a large bowl, whisk together the cake flour, cocoa powder, baking soda and salt.

In the bowl of a stand mixer or using a hand mixer, cream together the butter and the sugar until the mixture turns pale and fluffy, around 5 minutes.

Add the eggs, one at a time, being sure to scrape down the sides of the bowl with a spatula to ensure the mixture at the bottom of the bowl is fully incorporated.

Stir the vegetable oil into the egg mixture along with the vanilla extract, then the vinegar and red food coloring.

Add one-third of the dry ingredients, then half of the buttermilk. Repeat these steps, ending with the remaining dry ingredients. This will ensure your batter does not become curdled.

Pour an equal amount of batter into the two cake pans and bake for 30 to 35 minutes, or until you can insert a skewer or toothpick into the cake and no cake crumbs stick to it.

As the cakes cool, prepare the frosting. I cool my cakes on a wire rack, usually for at least an hour because they must be completely cool before frosting them.

(continued)

CREAM CHEESE FROSTING

8 oz (227 g; 1 block) cream cheese, at room temperature

½ cup (114 g; 1 stick) butter, softened

3½ cups (420 g) powdered sugar

1 tsp vanilla extract

To make the frosting, in the bowl of a stand mixer or using a hand mixer, whip the cream cheese with the butter, constantly scraping down the bowl, around 3 minutes.

Gradually add the powdered sugar, a few spoonfuls at a time, to prevent the powdered sugar from spilling all over the counter (I learned this from several kitchen clean-ups). Finish by adding the vanilla.

When the cakes are completely cool, remove them from the pans. Spread some cream cheese frosting on top of the first cake layer, and top with the second layer of cake. Spoon the rest of the frosting on top of the cake and use a spatula to spread the frosting around the top. If you'd like to frost the sides of the cake, double the frosting recipe. It is traditional to decorate red velvet cakes with red velvet cake crumbs. To do this, just crumble up any excess cake (maybe from leveling the cakes or from the pan) and sprinkling the crumbs on top of the cake and around the bottom edges to form an elegant, simple garnish.

NOTES:

See page 11 to learn how to make your own cake flour and buttermilk.

You can customize this frosting! In the kitchen, sometimes you have to improvise. Because you do not bake this frosting, the ratio of ingredients can be changed! If you like your frosting sweeter/less sweet, add more/less sugar! If you want an extra "tang," add 1 oz (28 g) of extra cream cheese. The original recipe, of course, won't let you down either ;)

VERY STRAWBERRY CUPCAKES WITH STRAWBERRY FROSTING

YiELD: 2 dozen cupcakes

DiFFiCULTY: 🍴🍴

There is nothing more satisfying than seeing a visually appealing dessert that tastes as good as it looks. With this strawberry cupcake recipe, the goal is to have a vibrant color of cupcake that you want to devour, with the flavor matching the expectation. These cupcakes are fruity, light and so much fun!

CUPCAKES

3⅓ cups (400 g) cake flour (see Note)

½ tsp baking soda

1½ tsp (7 g) baking powder

¼ tsp salt

1 cup (227 g) unsalted butter

1¾ cups (350 g) sugar

2 eggs

4 egg whites (see egg-separating tips on page 10)

1 cup (165 g) chopped fresh or frozen (thawed) strawberries, plus ¾ cup (130 g) diced fresh strawberries, divided

½ cup (120 ml) buttermilk (see Note)

1 tsp vanilla

Red food coloring (optional)

Preheat the oven to 350°F (175°C). Line 24 cupcake tins with cupcake liners.

To make the cupcakes, in a large bowl, whisk together the cake flour, baking soda, baking powder and salt.

In the bowl of a mixer or using a hand mixer, beat the butter and sugar together until the mixture becomes super creamy and white. One by one, mix in the eggs, then the egg whites.

Place the strawberries into a blender or food processor and blend the strawberries until they turn into a liquid with no more chunks, 3 to 4 minutes. This technique is called puréeing. Measure out ⅔ cup (160 ml) of the strawberry purée and add it to a bowl. If you have any left over, save it for another use. Add the buttermilk and vanilla to the strawberry purée.

Add one-third of the dry ingredients to the butter and egg mixture, then add half of the buttermilk–strawberry mixture. Repeat this step, ending with the last one-third of the flour mixture. Always mix your cake batter on low speed to avoid overmixing the batter! This ensures your cake crumb will be soft and delicate.

When the mixture is fully combined, or as pro bakers say, "homogenous," gently stir in the diced fresh strawberries and red food coloring (if using).

Spoon an even amount of batter into each cupcake liner. The trick is to fill the liners about three-quarters full of batter. If you fill them to the top, the tops will spread and be too wide to frost, but if you don't fill them enough, they won't have that perfect round top. Bake the cupcakes for 20 to 25 minutes, until a toothpick inserted into the center of the cupcake comes out clean. Allow the cupcakes to cool completely.

(continued)

FROSTING

½ cup (114 g; 1 stick) butter, softened

8 oz (227 g; 1 block) cream cheese, at room temperature

3½ cups (420 g) powdered sugar

2 tbsp (40 g) seedless strawberry jam

1 tsp vanilla extract

1 cup (20 g) freeze-dried strawberries or 1¼ cups (180 g) fresh strawberries, chopped

Red food coloring

To make the frosting, in the bowl of a stand mixer or using a hand mixer, whisk together the butter and cream cheese on high speed, around 3 minutes. Add the powdered sugar on low speed, little by little, to avoid all of it flying out of the bowl! Be sure to pause and scrape down the sides of the bowl a few times to ensure the frosting is evenly mixed. Stir in the strawberry jam and vanilla.

If you are using freeze-dried strawberries, blend the strawberries using a blender or food processor until the strawberries are a fine powder. For a smoother buttercream, push the strawberry powder through a sieve to remove any seeds. If you are using fresh strawberries, purée the strawberries in a blender. Place them in a pot, then place the pot on the stove on a medium-low heat setting. Stir constantly until the mixture starts to thicken. The strawberries should reduce to a few tablespoons of liquid, almost a jam consistency. This should take about 15 minutes. Pour into a heat-safe bowl and refrigerate until fully cooled.

Stir the strawberry powder, or strawberry purée, and red food coloring into the frosting.

To assemble the cupcakes, place a piping tip on a piping bag and use scissors to cut a hole that tightly holds the piping tip. To fill the bag, place the bag into a drinking glass and open the bag. Open the bag around the glass and fold the edges of the bag over the glass to hold it open. Spoon the frosting into the bag then remove the bag from the glass. Hold the bag with two hands, with your dominant hand on the bottom. Apply light pressure from your dominant hand, guiding the frosting in a circle onto the cupcake. This technique is known as piping.

If you don't have a piping bag, you can use a sandwich bag. Cut a small incision in one of the bottom corners of the bag. Fill the bag with frosting and use the same technique as the piping bag technique.

NOTE: To make your own cake flour or buttermilk, see page 11.

iMMACULATE ANGEL FOOD CAKE

Angel food cake is one of my favorite desserts from childhood (even though I'm only 16!). My grammy would also serve an angel food cake with strawberries in the summertime and the thought of that flavor combination instantly fills me with nostalgia and happy memories. That is exactly what angel food cake does; one bite puts a wide smile on your face. Though the ingredients are simple, the technique required is a bit tricky. So, roll back your sleeves and put your best chef hat on. We're here to get better, after all! There are only a handful of ingredients in an angel food cake, but that simplicity is exactly what makes it so magical. It's a dessert fit for the heavens!

YiELD: One 10-inch (25-cm) cake

DiFFiCULTY: 🥄🥄🥄

12 egg whites (see egg-separating tips on page 10)

2 tsp (9 g) cream of tartar (see Notes)

2 tsp (10 ml) vanilla extract

1¼ cups (150 g) cake flour (see Notes)

1¾ cups (350 g) granulated sugar

½ tsp salt

Berries, for garnish (optional)

Powdered sugar, for garnish (optional)

NOTES:

Cream of tartar can be found in the spice aisle of the grocery store.

To make your own cake flour, see page 11.

Before beginning the recipe, I recommend allowing your egg whites to rest outside the refrigerator until they come to room temperature. The egg whites will whip up quicker if they are at room temperature and the cake will bake more evenly.

Preheat the oven to 350°F (175°C) and get a 10-inch (25-cm) tube pan.

In the bowl of a stand mixer or using electric beaters, whip the 12 egg whites with the cream of tartar and vanilla until soft peaks form, about 5 minutes in a stand mixer. Soft peaks refers to the texture of the egg whites. When you remove the whisk from the bowl, the egg whites should be soft and form a beak shape on the whisk attachment.

Sift together the cake flour, sugar and salt. Pour a little bit of the dry ingredients over the egg whites and, using a spatula, very gently fold in the dry ingredients. Repeat this process until there is no more flour. The technique of "folding" simply means scooping the egg whites from the bottom of the bowl to the top of the bowl, being very gentle. We don't want to deflate the air by simply stirring the mixture. Once the flour is completely incorporated, carefully spoon the batter into an ungreased tube pan. By leaving the pan ungreased, the egg whites can cling to the edges of the pan and make the cake super soft.

Bake on the lowest rack of the oven for 40 to 45 minutes, or until you can insert a toothpick into the cake and it comes out clean. Immediately after removing the pan from the oven, flip the pan upside down to let it cool. When the cake comes out of the oven, it is still very soft, and cooling it upside down prevents the cake from collapsing. Let the cake cool completely; this could take a few hours. When it is completely cool, run a knife through the edges and release the cake. Serve with berries and powdered sugar, if desired. Enjoy a dessert fit for an angel!

PERFECT POUND CAKE WITH LEMON GLAZE

YIELD: One 10-inch (25-cm) cake

DIFFICULTY: 🥄🥄

One of my earliest memories of baking was learning how to make pound cake in kindergarten. Though I don't remember a whole lot of that day (being 5 years old), I remember the way baking made me feel; the sense of fulfillment from knowing I made a delicious cake with my own hands (and several other helping hands . . .) stuck with me. In short, if a kindergartener could do it, so can you!

Legend has it that pound cake originated by mixing a pound of each ingredient together, so it's safe to say this cake is on the heavier side. I recommend serving it with whipped cream and berries.

POUND CAKE

Cooking spray

8 oz (227 g; 1 block) cream cheese, at room temperature

1½ cups (341 g; 3 sticks) butter, at room temperature

3 cups (600 g) granulated sugar

6 eggs

2 tsp (10 ml) vanilla

3 cups (375 g) all-purpose flour

LEMON GLAZE

2 cups (240 g) powdered sugar

¼ cup (60 ml) lemon juice

1 tbsp (14 g) butter, melted

½ tsp vanilla extract

Preheat the oven to 325°F (165°C) and spray a 10-inch (25-cm) tube pan or a large Bundt pan with cooking spray or brush with butter, being sure that you reach all the crevices if using a Bundt pan.

In the bowl of a stand mixer or a large bowl, using a hand mixer, whip the cream cheese and butter together, around 6 minutes. On low speed, add the sugar little by little, then beat for another 8 minutes, until super light and fluffy. This process may seem time consuming, but the difference in the final product is so worth it.

Add the eggs, one at a time, mixing after each and scraping down the bowl with a spatula every so often to ensure all the ingredients are thoroughly combined.

Mix in the vanilla, then add all the flour in one incorporation. Mix until there are no more lumps in the batter but be sure not to mix it too much because you don't want the cake to be tough!

Pour the batter into the prepared pan and bake for 1 hour and 20 minutes on the middle rack. At 1 hour, check the cake by sticking a toothpick into the center. By 1 hour and 20 minutes, it should come out clean. Allow the cake to cool in the pan for about 30 minutes.

To make the glaze, in a large bowl, whisk together the powdered sugar, lemon juice, butter and vanilla. Mix until smooth. If there are lumps, microwave the mixture in 30-second increments, stirring after each time, until no clumps of sugar remain.

When the cake is fully cooled, invert the cake tin onto a plate or cake stand to release. Drizzle the top with the lemon glaze and enjoy!

BERRY BLAST CUPCAKES

At a first glance, these cupcakes seem like a delicious white cupcake, but when you bite into them, there is a surprise pop of red raspberry filling. This dessert will give you training in flavor combinations. Pairing lemon with raspberry, as in this cupcake, is always a good idea. The star of the show is the lemon cream cheese buttercream. It is such a unique flavor that you won't find it just anywhere. Tasting it for the first time was a revelation. I think I transcended when I ate it. These cupcakes have literally been described as "the best cupcakes I have ever tasted in my life," so I think it's safe to say these are a must-try. These cupcakes are a labor of love but so incredible and worth every second. The flavor is just immaculate.

YiELD: 2 dozen cupcakes
DiFFiCULTY: ♪ ♪

CUPCAKES

3 cups (375 g) all-purpose flour

1 tbsp (14 g) baking powder

¼ tsp salt

½ cup (114 g; 1 stick) unsalted butter, at room temperature

1½ cups (300 g) granulated sugar

½ tbsp (8 ml) vegetable oil

4 eggs

Zest of 2 lemons

1 tbsp (15 ml) vanilla extract

¾ cup (180 ml) buttermilk (see Note)

½ cup (120 ml) freshly squeezed lemon juice

Line two muffin tins with cupcake wrappers. Preheat the oven to 350°F (175°C).

To make the cupcakes, in a large bowl, whisk together the flour, baking powder and salt.

In the bowl of a stand mixer fitted with a paddle attachment or using a hand mixer, cream the butter with the sugar and oil until the mixture is pale and fluffy, around 5 minutes. Add the eggs, one at a time, mixing after each and scraping down the sides of the bowl with a rubber spatula to ensure the ingredients are evenly incorporated. Then mix in the lemon zest and vanilla extract.

In a small bowl, mix the buttermilk and lemon juice.

Add one-third of the dry ingredients to the butter and sugar mixture and blend, then add half of the buttermilk-lemon mixture and blend again. Repeat these two steps, ending with the last one-third of the flour mixture. This will prevent the batter from curdling.

Fill the cupcake liners three-quarters of the way full of batter and bake for 25 to 30 minutes, or until you can stick a skewer or toothpick in the middle and it comes out clean. Set the cupcakes aside to cool in the tins for at least 1 hour.

(continued)

RASPBERRY CURD

16 oz (454 g) fresh raspberries

⅔ cup (132 g) granulated sugar

2½ tbsp (38 ml) lemon juice

4 egg yolks (see page 10 for egg-separating tips)

2 eggs

½ tsp salt

½ cup (114 g; 1 stick) unsalted butter

LEMON SYRUP

¼ cup (60 ml) water

¼ cup (50 g) sugar

2 tbsp (30 ml) lemon juice

LEMON CREAM CHEESE FROSTING

½ cup (114 g; 1 stick) unsalted butter, softened

8 oz (227 g; 1 block) cream cheese

3 cups (360 g) powdered sugar

2 tbsp (30 ml) freshly squeezed lemon juice

1 tsp vanilla extract

¼ tsp salt

For the raspberry curd, add the raspberries, sugar and lemon juice to a saucepan and place over medium heat. Stir the mixture until it begins to boil and the raspberries soften and break down.

Pour the raspberry mixture through a mesh sieve to remove the seeds. This step should leave you with 1 cup (240 ml) of raspberry liquid.

Add the cooked raspberry purée back to the saucepan along with the egg yolks, eggs and salt. Whisk over medium-low heat until the curd starts to thicken, 6 to 7 minutes. The mixture should reach 180°F (82°C) if you check with a food thermometer. Stir in the butter and continue stirring until the butter has melted completely.

Pour the curd into a bowl, cover with plastic wrap and refrigerate until thickened, around 3 hours. To speed up this process, pour the curd onto a cookie sheet, spread it very thin, cover with plastic and place in the freezer. You will have thickened curd in no time!

For the syrup, mix the water, sugar and lemon juice in a small saucepan and heat on medium just until the sugar dissolves, 3 to 5 minutes.

For the frosting, cream together the butter and cream cheese in the bowl of a stand mixer. Add the sugar, mixing well until everything is evenly distributed. Last, mix in the lemon juice, vanilla and salt.

To assemble the cupcakes, use a pastry brush to brush the top of each cupcake with lemon syrup. Using an apple corer (or the back of a piping tip, or even just a knife), make an incision through the center of the cupcake. Be careful, because you don't want to cut all the way to the bottom of each cupcake.

Place the raspberry curd into a piping bag or sandwich bag with a bottom corner cut off and fill the hole in each cupcake with the raspberry curd.

Finally, fill a piping bag fitted with a tip (the star tip is my favorite) and pipe the frosting onto the cupcakes. See page 25 for cupcake decorating tips.

NOTE: To make your own buttermilk, see page 11.

PiNEAPPLE UPSiDE-DOWN CAKE

The concept of a pineapple upside-down cake has always been fascinating to me; it's all about that dramatic reveal of the pineapple design when you flip the cake. My favorite pineapple upside-down cake is moist, fluffy and full of pineapple goodness. This recipe covers the basics of cake making and teaches you how to incorporate fruit into baked goods. I hope you love this recipe as much as I do.

YiELD: One 9-inch (23-cm) cake

DiFFiCULTY: 🥄🥄

1 (20-oz [567-g]) can sliced pineapple

1 (10-oz [284-g]) jar maraschino cherries

4 tbsp (56 g) butter, melted

½ cup (110 g) brown sugar

1½ cups (190 g) flour

1 tsp baking powder

¼ tsp baking soda

¼ tsp salt

⅓ cup (80 ml) milk

¼ cup (60 ml) sour cream

¼ cup (60 ml) canned pineapple juice

1 tsp vanilla

½ cup (114 g; 1 stick) butter, at room temperature

¾ cup (150 g) granulated sugar

2 eggs

Preheat the oven to 350°F (175°C).

Remove the pineapple from the can and the maraschino cherries from the jar. Pat them dry with a paper towel and set aside.

Pour the melted butter into an ungreased 9-inch (23-cm) round cake pan. Use a pastry brush (or just rotate the pan if you don't own a brush) to spread the butter all around the pan. Sprinkle the brown sugar atop the butter, making sure to spread it evenly.

Here comes the most difficult part of the whole process: laying out the pineapple (and it's not even that hard . . . I believe in you!). Layer the pineapple rings on top of the brown sugar. This process is a bit like a jigsaw puzzle. I usually place five pineapple rings on the edges of the pan and one in the center. Then, I slice the remaining circles in half and place them facing upright on the edges of the pan. Place a maraschino cherry in the middle of each full pineapple ring.

In a large bowl, whisk together the flour, baking powder, baking soda and salt.

In a second bowl, whisk the milk, sour cream, pineapple juice and vanilla together.

In the bowl of a stand mixer or using a hand mixer, cream together the butter and sugar until light and fluffy, around 6 minutes. Add the eggs, one at a time, mixing after each addition. Scrape down the edges and bottom of the bowl with a spatula after each egg to make sure the ingredients are evenly incorporated!

(continued)

Add one-third of the dry ingredient mixture to the butter and sugar and mix, then fully stir in half of the wet ingredients. Repeat these steps, ending with the rest of the dry ingredients. This way we make sure the batter isn't lumpy.

Gently spread the smooth batter atop the intricately placed pineapples in the pan.

Place the pan on a baking tray and slide both into the oven. Bake for 35 to 40 minutes, or until a toothpick inserted in the center of the cake comes out clean. If the cake is not done baking at 40 minutes, remove the cake from the oven, place a sheet of aluminum foil over the cake pan (be careful because the pan will be hot!), then bake for an additional 10 minutes. Check the cake again with a clean toothpick and if it comes out clean the cake is done. If not, return it to the oven with the aluminum foil on top, and bake for an additional 10 minutes, or until a toothpick comes out clean.

Let the cake cool for 30 minutes in the pan . . . and then comes the moment of truth (I get so excited for this part!). Run a spatula or knife down the edges of the cake and then flip the cake tin onto a serving plate. Lift the cake pan (the more dramatic the better) and BAM! This cake will surely impress anyone you serve it to (despite it being easier than it looks to make . . . but that's our secret).

SUNDAY MORNING COFFEE CAKE

Sundays are a bittersweet day for me. It's nice to sleep in, but then I realize I have homework. My solution? Procrastination baking. This coffee cake is tender, light and packed with incredible cinnamon flavor. It doesn't actually have coffee in it, rather it's usually served alongside a nice cup of coffee (or tea). This coffee cake is perfect for those days when you just need to stop and smell the flowers (and this incredible cake).

YiELD: One 9 x 13-inch (23 x 33-cm) coffee cake

DiFFiCULTY: 🥄🥄

Cooking spray

STREUSEL LAYER

1 cup (125 g) all-purpose flour

1 cup (220 g) dark brown sugar

1½ tsp (4 g) cinnamon

¼ tsp salt

½ cup (114 g; 1 stick) butter, slightly soft

CINNAMON SWIRL

¼ cup (50 g) granulated sugar

3 tbsp (42 g) brown sugar

1½ tbsp (12 g) flour

2 tsp (6 g) cinnamon

CAKE

3 cups (375 g) flour

2¼ cups (450 g) granulated sugar

¾ tsp baking powder

½ tsp baking soda

¼ tsp salt

1 cup (227 g; 2 sticks) butter, at room temperature

1 cup (240 ml) sour cream

¼ cup (60 ml) milk

4 eggs

2 tsp (10 ml) vanilla extract

Preheat the oven to 350°F (175°C) and spray a 9 x 13-inch (23 x 33-cm) baking dish with cooking spray or brush with butter on the bottom and all four sides.

Prepare the streusel topping by stirring the flour, brown sugar, cinnamon and salt in a large bowl. Slice the butter into chunks and add to the dry ingredients. Using your (clean!) hands, mix the butter into the sugar and flour mixture. If that technique is a bit too . . . rustic for your liking, you can use a wooden spoon. You want to create clumps that will crisp up on the top of the cake.

To make the cinnamon swirl, combine the granulated sugar, brown sugar, flour and cinnamon in a small bowl, being sure to whisk it to evenly incorporate all the ingredients.

To make the cake batter, combine the flour, granulated sugar, baking powder, baking soda and salt in the bowl of a stand mixer or in a large bowl with a hand mixer. Add the butter and mix on low speed to gradually incorporate the butter. Mix for 3 minutes.

In a small bowl, mix the sour cream, milk, eggs and vanilla.

Turn the mixer on low speed and stream in the milk mixture. Mix for about 3 more minutes, until there are few to no lumps of flour left.

Pour half of the batter into the prepared baking dish. Spread it out using a spatula to make sure the batter is evenly distributed. Sprinkle on the cinnamon swirl layer, being sure to cover the entirety of the batter. Top the cinnamon swirl layer with the rest of the cake batter, then sprinkle the streusel on top.

Place your masterpiece in the oven and bake for 1 hour, or until it passes the toothpick test (you can insert a toothpick into the cake and it comes out clean). If you insert the toothpick in the cake and it does not come out clean, put a piece of aluminum foil loosely on top of the pan and return it to the oven for an additional 10 minutes, or until it passes the toothpick test.

Let the cake come to room temperature in the pan on the counter (or just to "warm temperature" if you can't wait that long) and slice into squares.

MY FAMOUS BANANA BREAD

Words cannot express how much I love banana bread. Not only is it delicious and easy, but it is also the perfect way to get rid of those brown bananas. Obviously, we don't want to use moldy bananas, but brown bananas actually make for the best banana bread. They contain more sugar, creating a better flavor and texture. Personally, I believe banana bread should be a staple in every household. It is so simple yet fun to make, and . . . it is just the best. I love my banana bread with chocolate chips but you can customize this recipe; I've seen people add a handful of coconut, walnuts or pecans.

YiELD: One loaf

DiFFiCULTY:

Cooking spray

½ cup (114 g; 1 stick) butter, softened

¾ cup (150 g) sugar

3 riiiiipe bananas (the brown ones you forgot to eat!)

2 eggs

½ tsp vanilla extract

1½ cups (190 g) all-purpose flour

1 tsp baking soda

1 tsp cinnamon

½ tsp salt

1 cup (168 g) semi-sweet chocolate chips (optional)

1 cup (117 g) chopped walnuts (optional)

Preheat the oven to 350°F (175°C) and spray a 4 x 8–inch (10 x 20–cm) loaf pan with cooking spray or brush butter on the bottom and all sides.

In the bowl of a stand mixer or large bowl with a hand mixer, cream the butter and sugar together until it becomes pale and fluffy, about 6 minutes.

Peel the bananas and place them in a shallow bowl. I find the best way to mash the bananas is with a fork and good ol' fashioned elbow grease. I take this as a time to "get my anger out" and go to town on the bananas. Once they are completely mashed (it's OK if there are few lumps), you're good to go.

Crack the eggs into the butter mixture and mix just until the eggs are incorporated. Scrape down the edges of the bowl with a spatula then add the mashed bananas and vanilla. At this point, your batter may look very curdled and separated. That is perfectly OK. The flour will bind the mixture together.

In a separate bowl, whisk the flour, baking soda, cinnamon and salt together, then add to the batter and mix just until combined. If desired, finish by mixing the chocolate chips and walnuts in by hand. Be sure to mix by hand to ensure we don't overmix the banana bread batter, which would make the bread overly dense.

Bake for 55 minutes to 1 hour. Remove the bread from the oven and stick a toothpick in it; if it comes out clean the bread is done. If it doesn't come out clean, add a sheet of foil to the top of the pan and bake for an additional 10 to 15 minutes, or until the bread passes the toothpick test.

Let the cake cool completely before serving.

SOUTHERN CARAMEL CAKE

Southern caramel cake is loved for its incredible flavor, but is notorious for being difficult to make. I was always intimidated by this cake because of its daunting reputation but it turns out the difficult part about this recipe is mainly the frosting. With the right equipment and mindset I *know* you can make this cake. You have the skills!! It requires speed and precision, but I promise, when done right, this southern classic is so worth it in the end.

YiELD: One 8-inch (20-cm) three-layer cake

DiFFiCULTY: ✏✏✏

CAKE

Cooking spray

1½ cups (190 g) all-purpose flour, plus more for the pans

1½ cups (180 g) cake flour (see Note)

1¼ tsp (6 g) baking powder

½ tsp salt

¾ cup (180 ml) sour cream

¼ cup (60 ml) buttermilk (see Note)

1 cup (227 g; 2 sticks) butter, at room temperature

1½ cups (150 g) granulated sugar

¾ cup (160 g) brown sugar, lightly packed

⅓ cup (80 ml) vegetable oil

6 eggs + 2 additional egg yolks (see page 10 for egg-separating tips)

1 tbsp (15 ml) vanilla extract

Preheat the oven to 350°F (175°C) and prepare three 8-inch (20-cm) cake pans by spraying the pans thoroughly with cooking spray or brushing with butter. Be sure to coat the edges to prevent sticking. Sprinkle a few tablespoons of flour into each pan, covering the edges with flour by rotating the pans. Discard any flour that does not stick. Preparing your cake pans this way will avoid any kitchen catastrophes!

In a large bowl, whisk the flour, cake flour, baking powder and salt. In another bowl, whisk the sour cream and buttermilk until evenly combined.

In the bowl of a stand mixer or a large bowl with a hand mixer, cream together the butter, sugar and brown sugar until the mixture becomes super fluffy, around 5 minutes.

Gradually stream in the vegetable oil with the mixer speed on low. When the oil is incorporated, crack in the eggs and the yolks one at a time, mixing after each and using a spatula to scrape down the edges and bottom of the bowl to ensure the ingredients are fully incorporated. Then, stir in the vanilla.

Add one-third of the dry ingredients to the butter mixture and mix until combined, then add half of the buttermilk mixture. Repeat these steps, ending with the last one-third of the dry ingredients. This technique ensures the cake batter is nice and smooth.

Portion the batter evenly among the three prepared cake pans and bake for 20 to 25 minutes, or until the cakes pass the toothpick test (you can insert a toothpick into the center of the cakes and it comes out clean).

Invert the cakes on to a wire rack and allow them to cool completely.

(continued)

FROSTING

4 cups (800 g) granulated sugar

2 cups (480 ml) buttermilk (see Note)

2 cups (456 g; 4 sticks) butter

2 tsp (9 g) baking soda

½ tsp salt

1 tbsp (15 ml) vanilla extract

To make the frosting, take a deep breath and let's go! Add the sugar, buttermilk, butter, baking soda and salt to a large saucepan or pot. You want to use a large pot because the caramel may bubble up and burning hot sugar can give you some pretty gnarly burns.

Put the pan on the stove, turn the heat to medium and bring the mixture to a simmer, meaning that the liquid touching the sides of the pan starts to bubble (think of it as a light boil). It is completely normal for the caramel to bubble up. If you think the mixture is going to overflow, immediately remove the pan from heat, and once the mixture is settled, return it to the heat.

Next, insert a candy thermometer into the sugar syrup—and I *highly* recommend using one, as precision is key here. Cook the mixture until the temperature reaches 235 to 240°F (113 to 116°C). This temperature is known as the soft-ball stage. This means if you poured a drop of the mixture into a glass of cold water, it would form a squishy ball of sugary-goodness. If you don't have a candy thermometer, this is the way to test if the mixture is ready; grab a glass of ice water and keep dropping small amounts of the sugar mixture into the water until a soft ball forms at the bottom. Be careful not to let the mixture get too hot, because cooking it past 240°F (116°C) may result in grainy frosting.

When the mixture has reached the soft-ball stage, stir in the vanilla, then let it cool for 20 minutes. Then, using a hand mixer (or transferring the caramel frosting to a stand mixer), whip for 4 to 5 minutes, creating a super thick consistency. This frosting is a bit harder to handle than a standard buttercream but you will be rewarded for your work!

To assemble, place about ¾ cup (96 g) of the caramel frosting on the bottom layer of the cake, then add the second layer on top and then repeat with the third layer. Spread the remaining frosting on top and all around the sides of the cake. If you're struggling to spread the frosting, run your spatula under hot water for a few seconds, dry it off, and the heat from the spatula should make decorating a bit easier (especially if your spatula is metal).

NOTE: To make your own cake flour and buttermilk, see page 11.

MY GRANDMA'S ULTIMATE COCONUT CAKE WITH CREAM CHEESE FROSTING

YIELD: One 9 x 13–inch (23 x 33–cm) sheet cake

DIFFICULTY: 🥄🥄

This coconut cream cake is surely one of the most meaningful in this entire book. This recipe comes directly from my grandma on my mom's side, who we call "Bibi." Bibi grew up in Iraq and immigrated to the United States in the 1960s, picking up various home-cooking skills as she had kids. Surprisingly, the cooking gene skipped a generation, proven by both of my parents' . . . difficulties in the kitchen, but I love learning Bibi's recipes. No family Easter celebration would be complete without Bibi's coconut cake. The incredible moist flavor of the cake with the tangy frosting is "just fantastic," as she says. And it wouldn't be complete without her decorating with shredded coconut dyed green and jelly beans to look like an Easter egg hunt. My one condition on sharing this recipe is that you make it with love.

Cooking spray

2 cups (250 g) all-purpose flour, plus more for the pan

1 tsp baking soda

¼ tsp salt

1 cup (227 g; 2 sticks) butter, at room temperature

2 cups (400 g) sugar

5 eggs, separated (see page 10 for egg-separating tips)

1 cup (240 ml) buttermilk (see Note)

1 cup (100 g) shredded coconut, plus more for decorating

1 batch cream cheese frosting (see Everyone's Favorite Red Velvet Cake with Cream Cheese Frosting, page 20)

Green food coloring (optional)

Jelly beans (optional)

Preheat the oven to 350°F (175°C) and prepare a 9 x 13–inch (23 x 33–cm) baking dish by spraying the pan thoroughly with cooking spray or brushing with butter. Be sure to coat the edges to prevent sticking. Sprinkle a few tablespoons of flour into the pan, covering the edges with flour by rotating the pan. Discard any flour that does not stick. Preparing your pan this way will avoid any kitchen catastrophes!

In a large bowl, whisk together the flour, baking soda and salt.

In the bowl of a stand mixer or large bowl using a hand mixer, beat the butter, then gradually add the sugar, spoonful by spoonful. When all the sugar is added, beat for 5 more minutes, until the butter is pale and fluffy.

Add the egg yolks, one at a time, to the butter mixture (emphasis on one at a time; I got yelled at for adding them all at once a few years back!). Mix after each addition and scrape down the sides of the bowl with a spatula to ensure the ingredients are evenly combined.

Add one-third of the flour mixture to the butter mixture and mix to combine, then add half of the buttermilk. Repeat this process, ending with the remaining one-third of the flour mixture. Be sure to scrape the bottom of the bowl to get any butter that wasn't incorporated. Remove the bowl from the mixer and gently fold in the coconut.

(continued)

MY GRANDMA'S ULTIMATE COCONUT CAKE WITH CREAM CHEESE FROSTING (CONT.)

NOTE: To make your own buttermilk, see page 11.

In another bowl, using a stand mixer or hand mixer, whip the egg whites until they reach stiff peaks (see the Light n' Fluffy Chiffon Cake with Whipped Cream recipe on page 51).

Pour the egg whites into the cake batter and very gently fold, being careful not to deflate the air we just whipped into the egg whites. The motion is to scoop from the top of the bowl to the bottom, then bringing the batter from the bottom to the top. This method of mixing ensures that the batter will remain fluffy but will incorporate the egg whites evenly.

Pour the cake batter into the prepared baking dish and bake for 40 minutes, or until you can insert a toothpick into the cake and it comes out clean.

Let the cake cool completely in the pan then invert the baking dish onto a serving tray.

To assemble, frost the entire cake with the cream cheese frosting. If you are decorating this cake for Easter, mix ½ cup (50 g) of shredded coconut with green food dye and sprinkle it on the cake to look like grass. Then top the cake with jelly beans to look like Easter eggs on the grass. While this decoration is perfect for an Easter celebration, it doesn't really work too often after that!

My favorite way of decorating this coconut cake for occasions other than Easter is with toasted coconut. I place ½ cup (50 g) of sweetened shredded coconut into a pan over medium heat and constantly stir until the coconut turns golden brown. Allow it to cool slightly, then sprinkle it over the cake. If you don't want to take the time to do that extra step, simply top the frosted cake with heaps of shredded coconut as a perfect alternative. Simple, quick and, most importantly, delicious!

MATTHEW-STYLE GERMAN CHOCOLATE CAKE

YiELD: One 9-inch (23-cm) two-layer cake

DiFFiCULTY: 🥄🥄

This is my spin on a traditional German chocolate cake. If you're unfamiliar with a German chocolate cake, it is a regular chocolate cake, but distinguished by its signature filling: a coconut and pecan filling unlike any other filling that exists! A moist, light-yet-rich cake is the trick to this recipe. This cake goes out to all of my fellow chocolate lovers.

CAKE

1 chocolate cake (from The Only Chocolate Cake You'll Ever Need with Swiss Meringue Buttercream, page 17)

COCONUT-PECAN FILLING

½ cup (114 g; 1 stick) butter, at room temperature

1 cup (220 g) brown sugar

3 egg yolks

1 (12-oz [354-ml]) can evaporated milk

1 tsp vanilla extract

1½ cups (150 g) shredded coconut

1 cup (109 g) chopped pecans

CHOCOLATE BUTTERCREAM

½ cup (114 g; 1 stick) butter, melted

⅔ cup (60 g) unsweetened cocoa powder

3 cups (360 g) powdered sugar

⅓ cup (80 ml) evaporated milk

½ tsp vanilla extract

½ tsp salt

Prepare the chocolate cake.

While the cake cools, make the filling. Add the butter, brown sugar, egg yolks, evaporated milk and vanilla to a large saucepan. Turn the heat on medium-low, and using a whisk, stir constantly. It's important to whisk the mixture well so the egg yolks are well mixed with the rest of the ingredients so they don't scramble as they heat. Whisk the mixture for 6 to 10 minutes, or until the mixture starts to become thick, almost the consistency of gravy.

Remove the pot from the heat and stir in the coconut and pecans then transfer that deliciousness to a heatproof bowl, cover the bowl with plastic wrap and place in the fridge until chilled.

To make the buttercream, add the melted butter and cocoa to the bowl of a stand mixer or a large bowl if you're using a hand mixer. Whisk thoroughly, doing your best to ensure there are no more clumps of cocoa. Add the powdered sugar very gradually, 1 cup (120 g) at a time, to prevent a massive mess. Then add the evaporated milk. Finish by stirring in the vanilla and salt, then we're ready to assemble.

Place one layer of cake on a serving tray, then spread a super thin layer of buttercream on the cake, then top with a heaping spatula-full of the gooey filling. Repeat with the next layer of cake. Frost the sides of the cake with the chocolate buttercream and place the remaining coconut filling on the top of the cake. It's a simple design, but shows the tasters exactly what kind of a treat they will soon eat.

VERY-BERRY STRAWBERRY CHEESECAKE

How does one even classify a cheesecake? Is it a cake? Is it a pie? While the answers to this question may be unclear, one thing is for certain: Cheesecake is absolutely delicious. The perfect, crispy graham cracker crust, topped with the decadent cheesecake base and served with a fresh strawberry topping is just unbeatable. In order to stay on top of the various components of this dessert, be sure to have all of your ingredients premeasured. This step will make your life way easier.

YiELD: One 9-inch (23-cm) cheesecake

DiFFiCULTY: ✎✎✎

GRAHAM CRACKER CRUST

10–12 graham crackers

3 tbsp (45 g) granulated sugar

1 tbsp (14 g) brown sugar

6 tbsp (84 g) butter, melted

CHEESECAKE FILLING

16 oz (454 g; 2 blocks) cream cheese, softened

2 tbsp (16 g) all-purpose flour

2 tsp (10 ml) vanilla extract

½ cup (120 ml) sour cream

1½ cups (300 g) sugar

2 tsp (10 ml) lemon juice

Zest of 1 lemon

3 eggs, at room temperature

Preheat the oven to 325°F (165°C) and grab a 9-inch (23-cm) springform pan. A springform pan is a cake tin with a removable bottom. You open the latch on the side of the cake pan, releasing the bottom of whatever dessert is in the pan. This way we can remove the cheesecake without fuss.

For the crust, place the graham crackers into a food processor and blend until they are fine crumbs. Measure out 1½ cups (150 g) of crumbs and add them to a large bowl along with the white and brown sugars and melted butter. Stir very well, incorporating all of the graham cracker crumbs into the butter, creating a sandy mixture.

Pour the graham cracker mixture into the springform pan and press the graham crackers into an even layer, then pack the crumbs up the sides of the pan. I do this step with my hands, but feel free to use a wooden spoon, or even the back of a measuring cup. You want the graham crackers pushed firmly into the bottom, then up the sides of the pan. When pushing the crust up the sides of the pan, the crust should only reach 1 to 2 inches (3 to 5 cm) up the side of the pan.

To make the cheesecake batter, in the bowl of a stand mixer or a large bowl using a hand mixer, beat the cream cheese. If you were making a cake, you would cream the butter and sugar together for several minutes, because it aerates the cake and creates a fluffy texture, but for cheesecake you want to do quite the opposite. Air inside of cheesecake batter will cause your cheesecake to crack. So, beat the cream cheese for only 20 to 40 seconds on medium speed to get rid of the lumps, but not whip air into the batter. Stir in the flour, just until combined, then mix in the vanilla, sour cream, sugar, lemon juice and lemon zest, for about 20 seconds.

Add the eggs, one at a time, and after adding each—and I know I sound like a broken record—don't mix any more than you need to evenly incorporate the egg. Be sure to scrape the edges of the bowl with a spatula after adding each egg!

(continued)

STRAWBERRY TOPPING

16 oz (454 g; 1 lb) fresh strawberries

⅓ cup (66 g) granulated sugar

2 tbsp (28 g) brown sugar

3 tbsp (45 ml) lemon juice

½ tsp vanilla extract

1½ tsp (4 g) cornstarch

2 tbsp (30 ml) water

Pour the batter into the graham cracker crust.

Wrap the bottom of the springform pan with foil. You should do this because no springform pan is 100% leak-proof . . . and the last thing you want is that creamy goodness spilling out of the pan!

One method that chefs swear by to prevent cracks in their cheesecake is baking the cheesecake in a water bath—inserting the springform pan into a baking dish that is filled with 1 inch (3 cm) of boiling water. The steam that the water creates allows the cake to rise without cracking. To use this method, place the foil-wrapped cheesecake in a 9 x 13–inch (23 x 33–cm) baking dish. Boil a pot of water on the stove and pour the boiling water into the baking dish (being careful not to pour any on the cheesecake!), surrounding the cake pan with water.

Bake for 55 to 65 minutes, or until the center of the cheesecake is just slightly jiggly. When done, turn off the oven, then open the oven door and let the cheesecake cool in that warm setting for an hour. Sharp changes in temperature can also cause the cheesecake to crack! Then place in the fridge for a minimum of 4 hours.

To make the strawberry topping, chop the stems off the strawberries, then cut them in half. Place the strawberries in a pot with the white and brown sugars, lemon juice and vanilla.

Stir constantly, and as the mixture heats up, the juices of the strawberries will be released. Stir until they start to break down, 8 to 10 minutes.

While the strawberries are cooking, make a slurry with the cornstarch and water. A slurry refers to mixing the cornstarch and water together before adding to the mixture you want to thicken. This skill prevents the cornstarch from clumping up in the topping. Stir the slurry into the strawberry mixture and cook for an additional 1 to 2 minutes, until the strawberries become nice and syrupy, almost like a thin jelly.

Top the semi-cooled cheesecake with the strawberries (which will conveniently cover any cracks that may have formed!) and refrigerate for 2 hours before serving.

To serve, run a knife around the edges of the springform pan and then release the bottom of the pan onto a serving tray. Slice and enjoy your beautiful strawberry cheesecake.

LIGHT N' FLUFFY CHIFFON CAKE WITH WHIPPED CREAM

YIELD: One 10-inch (25-cm) tube cake

DIFFICULTY: 🥄🥄

What exactly is a chiffon cake? For years, I referred to this cake as "the fluff cake" because it is so deliciously light. The trick that makes a chiffon cake different from a standard vanilla cake is that it uses whipped egg whites as the main leavening agent. In other words, the egg whites added to the baking powder and baking soda cause the cake to rise and become airy. Topped with a simple whipped cream, this recipe is perfect for the summer, or honestly any time.

CHIFFON CAKE

2 cups (240 g) cake flour (see Notes)

1½ cups (300 g) sugar

1 tbsp (14 g) baking powder

½ tsp salt

7 eggs, separated (see page 10 for egg-separating tips)

¾ cup (180 ml) water

½ cup (120 ml) canola oil

2 tsp (10 ml) vanilla extract

Zest of 1 lemon (optional)

½ tsp cream of tartar (see Notes)

Preheat the oven to 325°F (165°C). We will be using a 10-inch (25-cm) tube pan (see Notes) for this recipe. Leave the pan ungreased, as this will help the cake become fluffy.

In a large bowl, sift together the flour, sugar, baking powder and salt. Form a well in the center of the dry ingredients (a "well" is a fancy way to say make a hole in the center of the flour mixture).

In another bowl, whisk the egg yolks, water, oil, vanilla and lemon zest, if using, until smooth. Stir the wet ingredients into the well in the dry ingredients.

In the bowl of a stand mixer or using electric beaters, whip the egg whites with the cream of tartar until stiff peaks form. One of the challenges of this recipe is knowing when to stop beating the egg whites. When you lift the whisk from the bowl, the egg whites on the whisk should form a "peak," or something that resembles a bird beak. Make sure the mixture is firm, but do not whip it to the point where it is dry.

Fold the egg whites into the egg yolk–flour mixture in four increments. The technique of folding is super important to making sure the cake is beautifully fluffy. When you add the egg whites, push your spatula to the bottom of the bowl, being very gentle, then lift to the top. We don't want to deflate the egg whites!

Add the batter to the ungreased tube pan and bake on the bottom oven rack for 50 to 55 minutes, or until the top of the cake springs back if you poke it gently. After removing the cake from the oven, immediately flip it upside down to cool. This step will prevent the cake from collapsing. When it is completely cooled (30 minutes to 1 hour), slide a knife around the sides of the pan to release the cake.

(continued)

WHIPPED CREAM

2 cups (480 ml) cold heavy whipping cream

¼ cup (30 g) powdered sugar

1 tbsp (15 ml) vanilla extract

Berries, for garnish (optional)

To make the whipped cream, pop the bowl that you are using into the freezer for an hour before starting. This step is optional, but will speed up the process.

Whipped cream is super simple. Pour the cream into the bowl of a stand mixer, or use an electric mixer, then whip on high speed until the cream starts to thicken. Add the sugar and vanilla and whip until the mixture forms stiff peaks, approximately 5 minutes.

Spread the beautiful whipped cream atop your delicate chiffon cake. Sprinkle some berries on top if you'd like, and you're ready to enjoy this absolute masterpiece of a cake.

NOTES:

To make your own cake flour, see page 11.

Cream of tartar can be found in the spice aisle of the grocery store.

You should use a tube pan, which may be difficult to come by, for this recipe. A chiffon cake can be made in normal cake pans, but without the tube, it may not have the same airiness. If using round cake pans, you will need three 9-inch (23-cm) pans. I recommend placing a circle of parchment paper on the bottom of each pan.

WHAT'S iN THE COOKiE JAR?

My love of baking comes from the delicious baking genre that is cookie making. When I was *really* young (personally, I consider my current age of 16 still pretty young), my mom only made one thing in the kitchen: an assortment of Christmas cookies. The warm smell of cookies flooded the air, and it felt like Santa's workshop. I would beg my mom to let me stir the cookie dough. I was always fascinated by the oven, and I've been told that I used to play with the knobs while there were cookie trays in the oven, leading to several batches of charred gingerbread men. Through those experiences, I learned the magic of cookies. A cookie is simple, yet *everyone* loves them. This chapter is devoted to sharing the simplicity and unique flavor profiles of each cookie.

FIVE-STAR CHOCOLATE CHIP COOKIES

YiELD: 36 cookies

DIFFICULTY: ✎

I stand by the fact that chocolate chip cookies are the most elite dessert ever. There is something about a chocolate chip cookie that makes it the best. Maybe it's the caramelized flavor the brown sugar brings. Maybe it's the chocolate chips that melt in your mouth. I could go on and on about these cookies, but in short, they are just the gold standard. This recipe is the classic chocolate chip cookie everyone knows and loves. There's no funny business here like resting the dough overnight or difficult techniques, but the outcome is still so delicious. For a more advanced approach to this all-time favorite, check out my Fancy Chocolate Chip Cookies recipe on page 75.

3 cups (375 g) all-purpose flour

1 tsp baking soda

½ tsp baking powder

1 tsp salt

1 cup (227 g; 2 sticks) butter, at room temperature

1¼ cups (275 g) brown sugar (either light or dark will work)

¾ cup (150 g) granulated sugar

2 tsp (10 ml) vanilla extract

2 eggs

2 cups (336 g) semi-sweet chocolate chips

Preheat the oven to 375°F (190°C) and line two baking sheets with parchment paper.

In a large bowl, whisk together the flour, baking soda, baking powder and salt. Set the bowl aside.

In the bowl of a stand mixer or a large bowl using a hand mixer, beat the butter, brown sugar and granulated sugar together until the mixture becomes super light and fluffy, around 6 minutes.

When the butter is fluffy, add the vanilla extract and eggs. Beat on medium speed for another 2 to 3 minutes, being sure to scrape down the sides of the bowl with a spatula to incorporate all the ingredients. While you mix, enjoy the smell of the butter, sugar and vanilla—one of my ABSOLUTE favorite smells ever.

Dump in the dry ingredients and mix on low speed so the flour doesn't spill everywhere. Mix just until the dough comes together in a ball, then stir in the chocolate chips by hand. I know it's tempting, but don't snack on all the cookie dough! We need it for these cookies!

Drop 2 tablespoons (40 g) of cookie dough on your baking sheet to form each cookie. Allow 2 inches (5 cm) of space between each dough ball to prevent the cookies from sticking together.

Bake for 8 to 10 minutes, or until the tops start to turn golden brown. Remove the cookies from the baking sheet with a spatula and place on a wire cooling rack. These are best served with a glass of milk.

QUICK AND EASY NO-BAKE OATMEAL COOKIES

YiELD: Approximately 30 cookies

DiFFiCULTY: ✎

As the name suggests, these cookies are . . . well, "quick and easy." Despite their simplicity, they are absolutely scrumptious. In fact, our family named them "oatmeal chocolate yum-yums." While I'm not sure "yum-yum" is a professional baking term, it accurately describes just how amazing these cookies taste.

½ cup (114 g; 1 stick) butter

2 cups (400 g) sugar

½ cup (120 ml) milk

2 tbsp (11 g) unsweetened cocoa powder

½ cup (129 g) peanut butter

3½ cups (315 g) old-fashioned rolled oats

1 tsp vanilla extract

Grab a large baking sheet (the tray you bake cookies on) and place a large sheet of wax paper on top.

Add the butter, sugar, milk and cocoa to a saucepan and place over medium heat. Allow the butter to melt, and bring to a rolling boil, meaning large bubbles are rising to the surface continuously.

When the mixture is boiling, add the peanut butter, then the oats, then the vanilla. Stir together, then remove the pot from the heat.

Drop spoonfuls of the cookie dough onto the wax paper. The technique here does not have to be exact; the cookies can be as large or small as your heart desires.

Let the cookies cool for 20 minutes on the wax paper (waiting to dig in is definitely the hardest part!), and the cookies should harden. The last step is to enjoy these quick and easy "yum-yums."

EASY-PEASY PEANUT BUTTER COOKIES

These cookies could be the easiest dessert I've ever made. I posted this recipe to my TikTok account, reaching 1.8 million views and generating thousands of testimonials from people enjoying these cookies. These could be the easiest baked goods you ever make, and perfect if you need your cookie fix in a pinch. I love eating these with ice cream!

YiELD: 1 dozen cookies

DiFFiCULTY: 🥄

1 cup (258 g) creamy peanut butter

¾ cup (150 g) sugar

1 egg

1 tsp vanilla extract (optional)

Preheat the oven to 350°F (175°C) and grab a large baking sheet. Cut a piece of parchment paper to approximately the same size and lay on top.

In a large bowl, stir together the peanut butter, sugar and egg (and vanilla if you want to elevate these to four-ingredient cookies).

When a solid dough has formed—after around 2 minutes of stirring—roll the dough into small spheres, about 1 inch (3 cm) in diameter.

Place the balls of dough onto the parchment paper–lined baking sheet with a few inches (5 cm) of space between each sphere, and flatten with a fork vertically, then horizontally, to create that infamous criss-cross pattern on top.

Bake the cookies for 10 to 15 minutes, until the tops of the cookies are golden brown. Remove them from the oven and let them cool for 10 minutes on a wire rack before eating. Personally, I love eating these with ice cream, or even drizzling melted chocolate on top. The possibilities are endless! I like to think of these cookies as a vessel for making a great dessert, because by themselves they are good, but because they only have three ingredients, they are best when complementing another sweet treat.

MARVELOUS MACAROONS

There is a very specific discussion we must have, and that is the difference between a macaroon and a macaron. A (coconut) macaroon is a small cookie made of coconut, while the (French) macaron (notice how it has one "o") is a sandwich cookie made of two meringue shells with some sort of filling between (the recipe for My Food Network–Winning S'mores Macarons can be found on page 70). In this recipe we're making delectable coconut macaroons. They are soft, delicate and shockingly easy to make!

YiELD: 2 dozen macaroons

DiFFiCULTY: ✎

1 (14-oz [396-g]) bag sweetened, flaked coconut

7 oz (¾ cup + 2 tbsp; 207 ml) sweetened condensed milk

¼ tsp salt

1 tsp vanilla extract

¼ tsp almond extract

2 egg whites (see page 10 for egg-separating tips)

5 oz (heaping ¾ cup; 141 g) semi-sweet chocolate chips

Preheat the oven to 350°F (175°C) and line two baking sheets with parchment paper.

Stir together the coconut, condensed milk, salt and vanilla and almond extracts in a large bowl.

In the bowl of a stand mixer with a whisk attachment or with a hand mixer, whip the egg whites until stiff peaks form (see more about this in my Light n' Fluffy Chiffon Cake with Whipped Cream recipe on page 51), 2 to 3 minutes.

Pour the egg whites into the coconut mixture and fold gently until the ingredients are evenly combined.

I use small ice-cream scoops that hold 1½ tablespoons (30 g) of dough per scoop to portion out my cookies. Feel free to simply use a regular spoon to scoop out your cookies. Arrange them on a baking sheet, ½ to 1 inch (1.3 to 3 cm) apart so that the cookies don't stick to each other. Bake for 20 to 25 minutes, just until the edges of the cookies are beautifully golden brown.

Allow the cookies to cool on their baking sheets at room temperature for 20 minutes.

Finish off the cookies with a layer of chocolate. Melt the chocolate by adding the chocolate chips to a microwave-safe bowl and microwaving in 30-second intervals. Stir in between each time you heat the chocolate. This method of heating the chocolate is called tempering and will allow the chocolate to become hard at room temperature. Dip the bottom of each cookie into the melted chocolate and then place them back on the parchment paper. If you have remaining chocolate, add it to a sandwich bag with a corner cut off or a piping bag and drizzle the chocolate over the macaroons.

Enjoy your easy, delicious coconut macaroons.

SUPER SNICKERDOODLES

Snickerdoodles are one of those cookies that are best homemade and make you feel all warm and cozy inside. The crispy exterior matched with the soft and chewy interior and subtle cinnamon flavor makes for a cookie that will have people begging for seconds. This cookie recipe is unique because of the use of cream of tartar, which give these cookies a texture unlike anything you'll ever try.

YiELD: 2 dozen cookies

DiFFiCULTY: 🥄

COOKIES

2¼ cups (280 g) flour

1 tsp baking soda

2 tsp (9 g) cream of tartar (see Note)

½ tsp salt

1 cup (227 g; 2 sticks) butter, at room temperature

1¼ cups (250 g) granulated sugar

2 eggs

2 tsp (10 ml) vanilla

CINNAMON-SUGAR TOPPING

3 tbsp (45 g) granulated sugar

1 tbsp (8 g) cinnamon

Preheat the oven to 350°F (175°C) and line a large baking sheet with parchment paper.

In a large bowl, whisk together the flour, baking soda, cream of tartar and salt.

In the bowl of a stand mixer or a large bowl using a hand mixer, cream together the softened butter and sugar until pale and fluffy, 4 to 5 minutes.

One at a time, crack in the eggs, mixing after each addition and scraping down the edges of the bowl with a rubber spatula after each egg. Then stir in the vanilla.

Add the dry ingredients to the butter mixture then mix on low speed until all the flour is incorporated.

To make the topping, in a small bowl, whisk together the granulated sugar and cinnamon.

Roll the snickerdoodle dough into little spheres, about 2 inches (5 cm) in diameter. Roll the dough in the cinnamon-sugar mixture, and arrange on the baking sheet. Make sure there is at least 2 inches (5 cm) of space between each dough ball!

Bake for 9 to 12 minutes, until the cookies become nice and golden. You definitely don't want to overbake these cookies, as they are meant to be soft and pillowy.

Serve these delicious cookies, then prepare to be wowed by the exceptional flavor and texture.

NOTE: Cream of tartar can be found in the spice aisle of the grocery store.

DECADENT DOUBLE CHOCOLATE CHIP COOKIES

YiELD: 16 cookies

DiFFiCULTY:

The best way I can describe these cookies is a brownie in cookie form. They are irresistible, chewy and, best of all, super decadent. These cookies don't require any advanced techniques, but you'd never be able to tell because of their amazing flavor.

1 cup (125 g) all-purpose flour

¼ cup (22 g) unsweetened cocoa powder

½ tsp baking powder

½ tsp salt

½ cup (114 g; 1 stick) butter, softened

8 oz (227 g) semi-sweet chocolate chips, plus ½ cup (84 g) for the dough (optional)

1 tsp vanilla extract

2 tsp (4 g) instant espresso powder or instant coffee granules (optional; see Note)

2 eggs

½ cup (100 g) granulated sugar

¾ cup (165 g) light brown sugar

Sea salt, for garnishing

NOTE: Adding espresso powder is a great way to enhance chocolate flavor without adding the taste of coffee. It can be omitted from the recipe if you don't have it or can't easily find it in a store.

Line two baking sheets with parchment paper.

In a small bowl, stir together the flour, cocoa powder, baking powder and salt.

Place the butter in a saucepan over medium heat and stir until it is melted. When the butter begins to simmer, remove the pan from the heat and whisk in the chocolate chips, vanilla extract and espresso powder (if using). Remove the pan from the heat and let the mixture cool.

While the chocolate mixture cools, add the eggs and the white and brown sugars to the bowl of a stand mixer fitted with the whisk attachment or a large bowl if you're using a hand mixer. Beat the eggs and sugar on high speed until the eggs turn a pale yellow, around 6 minutes. Turn the mixer to low speed and carefully pour in the cooled chocolate mixture (or add the chocolate spoonful by spoonful if you don't have a mixer).

Remove the bowl from the mixer, then pour the dry ingredients into the bowl. Fold the flour in, very lightly, being careful not to deflate the air we whipped into the eggs. Here's your reminder that folding means using a rubber spatula or wooden spoon to gently mix in the ingredients without deflating the batter. Scoop the batter from the bottom to the top, stirring in a circular motion.

When the batter comes together, I always toss ½ cup (84 g) of extra chocolate chips, just because there's never too much chocolate. Cover the bowl with plastic wrap and let it sit at room temperature for 30 minutes. The batter will be much looser than a standard cookie dough!

While the dough is chilling, preheat the oven to 375°F (190°C).

Scoop 1 tablespoon (20 g) of batter per cookie onto your prepared baking sheets, with 2 inches (5 cm) between each cookie. Bake for 9 to 12 minutes, or until the tops are beautifully crinkled. Top with a sprinkle of sea salt and enjoy!

NOT-YOUR-AVERAGE OATMEAL RAISIN COOKIES

YiELD: 2 dozen cookies

DiFFiCULTY: ✐

To be frank, I hate raisins. The texture, the flavor . . . both just are not my favorite, and actually I've got to say one of my least favorites. For a long time, I could not understand why people would dare to bake with old, wrinkly grapes. I would never even touch an oatmeal raisin cookie. But, after picking up an oatmeal raisin cookie thinking it was a chocolate chip cookie, to my shock, it turned out I actually enjoyed the flavor of the cookie, and even the sweetness from the raisin. That's where the idea for this recipe came from. With a few extra special ingredients, I created a cookie that I was excited to eat *even though* it has raisins in it.

1 cup (125 g) all-purpose flour

1 tsp cinnamon

½ tsp baking soda

¼ tsp salt

1½ cups (135 g) old-fashioned rolled oats

½ cup (114 g; 1 stick) butter, softened

½ cup (110 g) brown sugar (I use dark brown sugar, but light works)

¼ cup (50 g) granulated sugar

1 egg

2 tsp (10 ml) vanilla extract

¼ cup (36 g) raisins

¼ cup (40 g) dried cherries, chopped into small pieces

½ cup (84 g) semi-sweet chocolate chips

Line two baking sheets with parchment paper.

In a large bowl, whisk together the flour, cinnamon, baking soda, salt and oats, then set aside.

In the bowl of a stand mixer or a large bowl (if using a hand mixer), beat the butter, brown sugar and granulated sugar together. Cream together for 4 to 5 minutes, until the mixture is light and fluffy.

Crack in the egg and mix, scraping down the sides of the bowl with a rubber spatula. Then, stir in the vanilla.

Dump the dry ingredients into the butter mixture and stir on low speed until a beautiful dough forms. Pour in the raisins, dried cherries and chocolate chips. I stir the mix-ins by hand to make sure I don't overmix the batter. Refrigerate the dough for 30 minutes to 1 hour.

While the dough is chilling, preheat the oven to 350°F (175°C).

Portion out 2 tablespoons (40 g) of dough per cookie and roll into a ball. Arrange on the baking sheets, then apply a tiny bit of pressure to the top of each dough ball to just slightly flatten each cookie.

Bake for 9 to 12 minutes, and there we have oatmeal raisin cookies, but taken up a notch.

MY FOOD NETWORK-WINNING S'MORES MACARONS

YiELD: 20 macarons
DiFFiCULTY: ✐✐✐

Don't be fooled! The notoriously difficult French macarons seem shockingly simple from their brief list of ingredients, but these delicate sandwich cookies are all about having the proper technique. Making this recipe, you will master the art of the meringue, as well as the proper way to fold the dry ingredients into a batter. The perfect macaron has a smooth top and "foot," or crowned edge around the bottom of each cookie.

CHOCOLATE SHELLS

1¾ cups (210 g) powdered sugar

¼ cup (22 g) cocoa powder

1 cup (95 g) almond flour/almond meal

3 egg whites (see Note)

⅓ cup (66 g) granulated sugar

NOTE: In this recipe it's particularly important that when separating the egg whites from the yolks, the yolk doesn't break open and mix with the whites! See page 10 for egg-separating tips.

Line a baking tray with parchment paper. To make the chocolate shells, in a bowl, whisk together the powdered sugar, cocoa powder and almond flour. Pour the mixture through a sieve to remove any lumps. For the best results, repeat this process twice! Set aside.

Place the egg whites in the bowl of a stand mixer, or a large bowl if using a hand mixer. For this recipe I recommend using an electric mixer or else your arms will get tired! Using a whisk attachment (or just a whisk), whip your egg whites. When they are frothy, start gradually sprinkling in the sugar, about 1 teaspoon at a time. Your meringue is ready when the mixture reaches stiff peaks (see the Light n' Fluffy Chiffon Cake with Whipped Cream recipe on page 51 for more information).

Pour half of the dry ingredients into the meringue mixture. Gently fold the batter using a rubber spatula, being sure to scrape the bottom of the bowl and not deflate the egg whites. When combined, add the rest of the dry ingredients and fold until the batter resembles molten lava and forms ribbons when dripped off the spatula.

Place the batter into a piping bag lined with a round tip, or a ziptop bag with a bottom corner cut off. For the best use of the piping bag, place your non-dominant hand above your dominant hand, which you should use to guide the batter. Apply pressure, being sure to keep your bag still, and squeeze the batter onto the prepared baking tray. For the best macarons, they should each be about 1½ inches (4 cm) in diameter. Be sure to leave about 1 inch (3 cm) of space in between, as the batter will spread slightly.

Lift the baking tray and hit it against the counter. This step may seem strange, but it will get rid of any air bubbles stuck inside the macaron batter. Let the shells rest for 30 minutes to 1 hour. During this time, preheat the oven to 300°F (150°C). Bake the macarons for 15 to 20 minutes, until they easily peel off the parchment paper. Let the shells cool on a wire rack or cookie sheet for 10 to 15 minutes.

MARSHMALLOW BUTTERCREAM

½ cup (114 g; 1 stick) butter

3 oz (85 g) cream cheese

½ cup (48 g) marshmallow fluff

½ cup (60 g) powdered sugar

½ tsp vanilla

Graham cracker crumbs, for garnish

To make the marshmallow buttercream, in the bowl of a stand mixer or a large bowl using a hand mixer, cream the butter, cream cheese and marshmallow fluff for 1 minute. Add the powdered sugar and vanilla and stir until fluffy.

The most fun part of the macaron process is the assembly! Match each macaron shell with another one, as close to the same size as possible. Using another piping bag or ziptop bag, pipe about 2 teaspoons (5 g) of the marshmallow buttercream onto the center of one of the macarons. Gently press the second macaron on top, allowing for some frosting to protrude out of the side of the macaron. Dip the macaron edges in crushed graham crackers to garnish.

The best macarons are chilled in the fridge overnight (I put them in an airtight container) as this allows for the texture to develop.

The last step is to enjoy!

LIP-SMACKING SOFT SUGAR COOKIES

I have a confession. My absolute least favorite cookies of all time are the pink-frosted sugar cookies that every grocery store sells. I find the actual cookie part to be bland and dry. Plus, the frosting is always brittle and overly sweet, tasting like pure chemicals rather than a fresh cookie. *These* cookies will amaze you. I don't think I appreciated how delicious sugar cookies could be until I made this recipe. With the soft texture and the perfect ratio of frosting to cookie, you'll never go back to the store-bought version.

YIELD: 2 dozen cookies

DIFFICULTY: 🥄🥄

COOKIES

1¾ cups (220 g) all-purpose flour

1½ tbsp (12 g) cornstarch

½ tsp baking powder

½ tsp baking soda

¼ tsp cream of tartar (see Note)

¼ tsp salt

½ cup (114 g; 1 stick) softened butter

¾ cup (150 g) granulated sugar

1 egg

2 tsp (10 ml) vanilla extract

⅓ cup (80 ml) sour cream

FROSTING

½ cup (114 g; 1 stick) butter, softened

2½ cups (300 g) powdered sugar

1 tbsp (15 ml) vanilla extract

1 tbsp (15 ml) milk

4–5 drops red food coloring

Rainbow sprinkles, for decoration

Line two baking sheets with parchment paper.

In a large bowl, whisk together the flour, cornstarch, baking powder, baking soda, cream of tartar and salt.

In the bowl of a mixer or a large bowl (if using a hand mixer), cream together the butter and sugar until the mixture becomes light and fluffy, around 5 minutes. Crack in the egg, pour in the vanilla and mix, then scrape the sides of the bowl with a rubber spatula. Then, stir in the sour cream.

Pour the dry ingredients into the butter mixture and mix on low speed until a dough forms, around 2 minutes.

Cover the bowl in plastic wrap and chill in the fridge for 1 to 2 hours. While the dough is chilling, preheat the oven to 350°F (175°C).

Roll 2 tablespoons (40 g) of dough into a ball and arrange on the baking sheet, allowing 2 inches (5 cm) of space in between each round of dough. Using the back of a spoon, lightly press on the tops of the cookies, slightly flattening them.

Bake the cookies for 9 to 12 minutes, just until the edges start to turn brown. We don't want these cookies to be golden; rather, they should be pale and pillowy.

To make the frosting, in the bowl of a stand mixer or a large bowl with a hand mixer, beat the butter for 3 minutes. Add the powdered sugar and mix, being sure to scrape the edges of the bowl with a spatula. Stir in the vanilla and milk, then the food coloring.

When the cookies are out of the oven, let them cool for 10 to 15 minutes on a wire rack or plate. To frost, use an offset spatula, or a butter knife, to spread 1 to 2 tablespoons (15 to 30 g) of buttercream atop the cookies. Top with sprinkles as the finishing touch.

Enjoy a delicious sugar cookie that is *way* better than anything you'll buy from the store!

NOTE: Cream of tartar can be found in the spice aisle of the grocery store.

FANCY CHOCOLATE CHIP COOKIES

Well, it's been established I am a sucker for the perfect chocolate chip cookie, and I think this has to be my favorite recipe. With a few tricks up my sleeve, I'm excited to share techniques that will amaze anyone who tastes your creations. The (not-so) secret ingredient is brown butter, which we make by browning the milk fat in the butter (I know it sounds confusing but it's easier than you think!). It adds a beautiful nutty and rich flavor. This recipe definitely takes more effort and way longer to make than your average chocolate chip cookie, but it is so worth it.

YiELD: 2 dozen cookies

DiFFiCULTY: ✏️✏️✏️

1 cup (227 g; 2 sticks) butter

2¼ cups (280 g) all-purpose flour

1 tsp baking soda

1 tsp salt

1 cup (220 g) dark brown sugar

½ cup (100 g) granulated sugar

2 eggs

1 egg yolk (see page 10 for egg-separating tips)

½ tsp instant espresso powder

1 tbsp (15 ml) vanilla extract

1 cup (168 g) dark chocolate, chopped into chunks

1 cup (168 g) milk chocolate, chopped into chunks

Sea salt, for garnish (optional)

Line two large cookie sheets with parchment paper.

In this recipe, you melt the butter, but take it a step further by boiling it until the butter turns a beautiful amber color. There is definitely a fine line between brown butter and burnt butter, so this step requires your full attention.

Place the butter in a saucepan over medium-high heat. When the butter is completely melted, reduce the heat to medium. The butter will start bubbling vigorously. Stir constantly. After 6 to 8 minutes, depending on the size of your pot, your butter should turn brown. It may be hard to see the actual color of the butter because of the bubble on top of the mixture. Swirl the butter around the bowl to see more of the color, or scoop a spoonful of the mixture to check the color. Again, there is a fine line between brown butter and burnt butter so be careful. When the butter is brown, pour it into a bowl and place the bowl in the fridge until the butter comes to about room temperature. Do not use hot butter in this recipe, as it will ruin the texture of the cookies!

While the butter is cooling, in a large bowl, whisk together the flour, baking soda and salt.

In the bowl of a mixer or a large bowl if using a hand mixer, add the now room-temperature brown butter, dark brown sugar and granulated sugar. Cream together until the mixture turns super fluffy, around 6 minutes. The fluffier the butter and sugar, the better the texture of the cookie! Add the two whole eggs, one egg yolk, espresso powder and vanilla extract. At this stage the butter and sugar will smell INCREDIBLE.

(continued)

FANCY CHOCOLATE CHIP COOKIES (CONT.)

Pour the dry ingredients into the butter mixture and mix on low speed until a beautiful dough forms.

When I want to go the extra mile to make these cookies, I splurge on high-quality chocolate bars. I use a sharp knife and chop lengthwise, then vertically to create lots of small chocolate chunks. I use a mix of dark and milk chocolate to create the perfect bite, but truthfully, you can use 2 cups (336 g) of whatever small chocolate bits you'd like.

Stir the chocolate into the batter on low speed, though I always incorporate the chocolate by hand to not overmix the dough. Overmixing the dough will lead to denser cookies.

Portion out 2 to 3 tablespoons (40 to 60 g) of dough on your cookie sheet per cookie, leaving approximately 2 inches (5 cm) of space between each cookie.

Next, chill the cookie dough in the freezer for a minimum of 5 hours. I hear you, that is so long for a batch of chocolate chip cookies, but freezing the dough ensures these cookies are the perfect shape and texture. I usually pop 'em in the freezer overnight and bake them the next day.

When you are ready to bake, preheat the oven to 375°F (190°C). Once the oven is preheated, bake for 9 to 12 minutes, or until the cookies are beautifully golden brown. Garnish with sea salt, if using.

And after that work, you will have chocolate chip cookies that taste exquisitely gourmet.

CLASSIC SUGAR COOKIE CUTOUTS WITH ROYAL ICING

YIELD: Approximately three dozen 3-inch (8-cm) cookies

DIFFICULTY: ✐ ✐ ✐

I love seeing intricately decorated sugar cookies. What's even better than viewing these beautiful cookies is biting into one and having the cookie taste as good as the decorations look. This style of sugar cookie is called a "rolled cookie," because you make the dough, then roll it out and cut shapes, as opposed to dropping the dough on a cookie sheet and baking it. I'm going to go over a few tricks of the trade to have you making beautifully decorated cookies in no time! The icing on top of the cookies is called "royal icing" and is a special type of icing that hardens. The trick is getting the right consistency of icing for the cookies.

COOKIES

2¾ cups (345 g) flour, plus more for rolling out the dough

¾ tsp baking powder

1 tsp salt

1 cup (227 g; 2 sticks) butter, softened

1 cup (200 g) granulated sugar

2 eggs

1 tbsp (15 ml) vanilla extract

In a large bowl, whisk together the flour, baking powder and salt, then set it aside.

In the bowl of a stand mixer or large bowl if you're using a hand mixer, cream together the butter and sugar until the mixture becomes light and fluffy, around 5 minutes.

Add the eggs, one at a time, mixing after each and scraping the edges of the bowl with a rubber spatula to ensure all the ingredients are properly incorporated. Then, stir in the vanilla.

Dump in the dry ingredients and mix on low speed, just until a dough forms, 1 to 2 minutes.

Split the dough in half and form into equal-sized discs. Wrap each disc in plastic wrap and chill in the fridge for 3 hours. Personally, I'm impatient when it comes to waiting for dough to chill, but for this recipe, because you will be cutting out shapes from the dough, if it isn't properly chilled, the dough will spread when baking and the shapes will be distorted. So: patience!

When you remove the dough from the fridge, preheat the oven to 350°F (175°C) and line three baking sheets with parchment paper.

(continued)

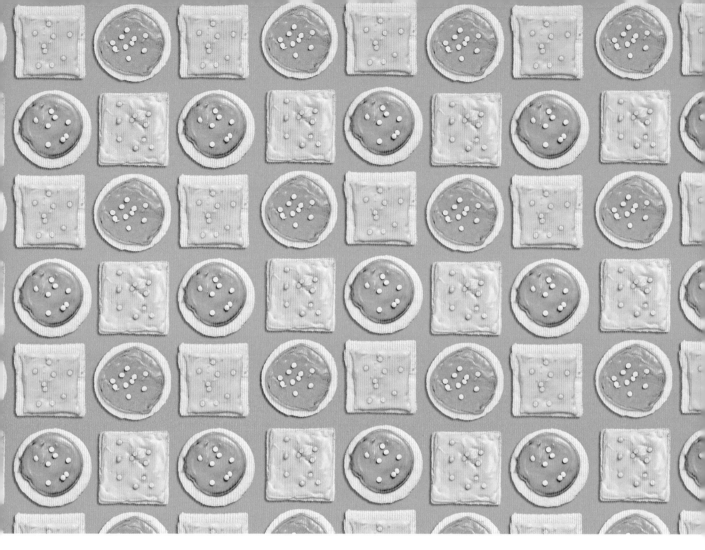

CLASSIC SUGAR COOKIE CUTOUTS WITH ROYAL ICING (CONT.)

You are going to roll the dough out on a counter, but to prevent the dough from sticking, you have to flour your surface, meaning sprinkle a light layer of flour where you want to roll the dough out so it doesn't stick. After flouring, roll out the dough to ½-inch (1.3-cm) thickness (or ¼ inch [6 mm] if you want crispier cookies). If your dough is too cold, it may be difficult to roll. Be patient, and allow it to soften slightly.

ROYAL ICING

4 cups (480 g) powdered sugar

3 tbsp (30 g) meringue powder

9–10 tbsp (135–150 ml) water

Food coloring

After rolling out the dough, use a cookie cutter to cut out your desired shapes. One area I've struggled in is moving the dough from the counter to the tray after cutting out the shape. That's why it is important to use cold dough! If your dough is stuck to the counter, use a metal spatula (one for flipping pancakes) and scrape gently to lift the cookie. After removing the cut-out shape, you will be left with a bunch of dough scraps. Gather them together into another pile of dough, then roll it again and cut out more shapes. Do not handle the dough more than needed; overworking the dough can cause the cookies to spread in the oven and lose their shape.

Place the cut-out cookies on the parchment paper and bake for 9 to 12 minutes, or until they just start turning golden brown. Remove the cookies from the oven and use a spatula to place the cookies on a wire rack to cool completely. While the cookies cool, prepare the icing.

To make the icing, in the bowl of a stand mixer with a whisk attachment (or even by hand), whisk the powdered sugar and meringue powder. Then, stir in the water. Whip on high speed until the frosting starts to look a bit fluffy. If you want to ice the cookies with multiple colors of frosting, portion the icing into separate bowls and stir in the food coloring of your choice into each bowl.

Decorating is both the most fun and the most challenging part, especially if you're attempting an intricate design. First, make sure your cookies are completely cool. If they are still warm they might melt the icing and you will get some strange-looking cookies. The standard way to decorate a cookie is to create a border of icing, and then flood the interior. This will make more sense in a second!

I highly recommend buying piping bags for this process. If not, you can use a sandwich bag and cut a tiny piece off one of the bottom corners. If using a piping bag, either use a really tiny piping tip or cut the end of the bag off toward the bottom, so only a thin stream of frosting can come out. Using the piping technique from the Very Strawberry Cupcakes with Strawberry Frosting recipe on page 25, pipe a thin line of frosting on the outer edges of the cookie. That's the border. Let that set for 5 minutes, then fill the cookie with frosting. Use a toothpick to evenly distribute the frosting. This technique is known as flooding the border.

Let the frosting sit for 30 minutes to 1 hour to let it fully harden, then voilà: ready to eat.

Of course, there are several other ways to decorate cookies, the easiest one being thinning out the icing with a tablespoon (15 ml) of more water, and simply dipping the cookie in the bowl of icing, then letting the cookie dry.

EASY AS PiE(S)!

Bakers! Welcome to Pie Making 101. Pies come in all different flavors, some being technically challenging and others are a piece of cake . . . or should I say slice of pie? By the time you bake your way through these delicious recipes, you'll be saying "that was as easy as pie." In this chapter, we cover the two main categories of pies: pies baked with the filling inside and pies that have their crusts baked before they are filled. The process of baking a pie crust before filling it, usually with some sort of custard, is called "blind-baking" and is a technique we will go over in this chapter. The one thing to understand about blind-baking is that you have to weigh the pie crust down using some form of weight, or the crust will shrink and leave you with a really sad-looking crust.

SIMPLE BERRY CRISP

A berry crisp is one of those desserts that is just so incredible, yet so simple. You just toss a few ingredients together, throw the tray in the oven, and BOOM, you have a warm dessert perfect for any occasion. This recipe doesn't require a whole lot of advanced skills, and the measurements for the berry filling don't have to be super exact, so there is wiggle room for your own spin on this recipe! Once you've mastered the original, try it with a new baking spice or even different combo of berries!

YIELD: One 9-inch (23-cm) crisp

DIFFICULTY: 🥄

FRUIT FILLING

2 cups (246 g) fresh raspberries

2 cups (288 g) fresh blackberries

2 cups (296 g) fresh blueberries

¼ cup (55 g) brown sugar

2 tbsp (16 g) cornstarch

2 tsp (10 ml) lemon juice

1 tbsp (8 g) flour

½ tsp cinnamon

CRISPY CRUMBLE

¾ cup (95 g) all-purpose flour

½ cup (45 g) old fashioned rolled oats

½ cup (110 g) brown sugar

½ cup (100 g) granulated sugar

½ tsp salt

½ cup (114 g; 1 stick) butter, cold, cubed

Ice cream, for serving

Preheat the oven to 350°F (175°C) and grab a 9-inch (23-cm) pie dish.

To make the filling, gently mix the raspberries, blackberries, blueberries, brown sugar, cornstarch, lemon juice, flour and cinnamon in a large bowl using a wooden spoon. Be sure to stir gently so you don't crush the berries! Pour the berry mixture into the pie dish.

To make the crumble, in a large bowl, combine the flour, oats, brown sugar, granulated sugar and salt. When the ingredients are well incorporated, add in the cold butter cubes. At this point, if you have a pastry blender, cut the butter into the flour mixture. If you don't have a pastry blender, use your fingers to press the butter into the flour mixture. Really work the butter in by mashing it in until the mixture becomes coarse crumbs.

Sprinkle the crumble over the fruit, then bake on a baking sheet for 1 hour, until the fruit becomes nice and bubbly around the top, and the crumble is golden. Scoop into bowls and serve with ice cream!

THE SECRET RECIPE KEY LIME PIE

Key lime pie gives off the best summer vibe because of its unique and almost tropical flavor. Just one bite transports me to the beach. In fact, I actually stumbled upon this recipe from a chef on one of my favorite vacations. With a few adaptations to the crust to make it simpler for budding chefs, this key lime pie is not technically too challenging, and although it is pretty simple to put together, it tastes like it came straight from the Florida Keys (where "Key" limes are originally from!).

YIELD: One 9-inch (23-cm) pie

DIFFICULTY: 🗝

CRUST

1 batch graham cracker crust (from the Very-Berry Strawberry Cheesecake recipe on page 49)

FILLING

3 egg yolks (see egg-separating techniques on page 10)

1 tbsp (6 g) lime zest

½ tsp vanilla extract

1 (14-oz [396-g]) can sweetened condensed milk

¾ cup (180 ml) Key lime juice (see Note)

1 drop green food coloring (optional)

Preheat the oven to 350°F (175°C). Prepare the crust recipe as written, but press it into a 9-inch (23-cm) pie dish, being sure to create an even coat of graham crackers on the bottom and sides of the dish. Bake the crust for 8 minutes.

While the crust is baking, make the filling. In the bowl of a large stand mixer with a paddle attachment, or a large bowl using a hand mixer, beat the egg yolks on high speed. Add the lime zest and vanilla. Mix on high speed until very pale and fluffy, around 5 minutes. With the mixer on low speed, slowly pour in the sweetened condensed milk. Scrape down the sides of the bowl with a rubber spatula, then beat on high speed for another 4 minutes. Turn the mixer off, then pour in the lime juice. At this point you can also add the green food coloring. In my opinion, one drop of green food coloring gives a key lime pie a fun tint of green that lets the tasters know the flavor and makes the dish fun! There are, of course, many key lime pie purists who are strongly opposed to the idea of food coloring in a key lime pie. Whichever direction you take, you'll have a delicious key lime pie! Mix on low speed just until the juice is incorporated, around 20 seconds.

Pour the lime deliciousness into that beautiful graham cracker crust and bake for 10 to 12 minutes, just until the center is set, or only slightly wobbly.

Let the pie cool for 15 minutes at room temperature, then refrigerate for a few hours, until it is completely cooled.

(continued)

WHIPPED CREAM

1 cup (240 ml) heavy whipping cream, very cold

3 tbsp (24 g) powdered sugar

2 tsp (10 ml) vanilla extract

While the pie is chilling, make the whipped cream. In the bowl of a stand mixer, add the cold cream. One helpful hint is to stick the mixing bowl into your freezer 30 minutes prior to making this recipe. Whip the cream using the whisk attachment (or use a hand mixer) for 1 to 3 minutes, just until stiffened. Add the powdered sugar and vanilla and mix just until combined.

When the pie is chilled, you can simply dump the whipped cream on the pie and spread it out, then serve, but if you want to be extra fancy, I recommend using a piping bag. See the Very Strawberry Cupcakes with Strawberry Frosting on page 25 for piping tips. For this pie, I fit my piping bag with a large star tip, then make a ring of whipped cream around the border of the pie, just to make the presentation really pop.

NOTE: Key limes are small limes, known for their tart and distinct flavor. They can be pretty tricky to find. If you can't find them at your local store, regular limes will do just fine. You can also buy bottled key lime juice, but that also might be tricky to find!

WHEN LIFE GIVES YOU LEMONS LEMON MERINGUE PIE

YIELD: One 9-inch (23-cm) pie

DIFFICULTY: 🥄 🥄 🥄

Lemon meringue pie has every element of the perfect dessert. It has the flaky, crispy crust, paired with the tart lemon curd filling, finished with a creamy swiss meringue. There are a few technical challenges in this recipe, like making a meringue or blind-baking (prebaking) a pie crust, but the challenges make for a delicious pie. The creamy lemon filling and the smooth meringue definitely will test your skills in the kitchen. Note that you will need a stand mixer for this recipe to make the meringue, so if you don't have one in your kitchen, bookmark this recipe for another day, or make it with a friend who has one in their kitchen.

CRUST

½ recipe pie crust (from All-American Apple Pie recipe, page 90)

LEMON FILLING

3 egg yolks (see egg-separating tips on page 10)

1½ cups (300 g) granulated sugar

⅓ cup + 1 tbsp (51 g) cornstarch

1½ cups (360 ml) water

1 tbsp (6 g) lemon zest

½ cup (120 ml) lemon juice

3 tbsp (42 g) butter

Preheat the oven to 450°F (230°C).

Following the instructions in the All-American Apple Pie recipe (page 90), roll out one disc of dough (one-half of the dough recipe) and place it in a 9-inch (23-cm) pie dish. Prick the crust with a fork, all over the bottom and sides of the dish. This technique is called docking the crust. Freeze the crust for 30 minutes. It is important to bake the crust while frozen. If it is not frozen solid or weighed down, the crust will puff up and sink into the pie dish, leaving you with a sad excuse for a crust. To anchor the crust, place a large sheet of foil on top of the pie crust, covering all the buttery goodness. Fill the crust with pie weights. I'd bank on the fact that most people don't own pie weights (even I don't own them), so I fill the pie crust with dry rice or dry beans. Bake the crust for 25 to 30 minutes, until the crust is golden brown. Remove the sheet of foil with the weight on top of it. After you remove the crust from the oven, reduce the oven temperature to 350°F (175°C). You have now prebaked the crust, which is known as blind-baking. You will be returning the crust to the oven, so it doesn't need to be cooked all the way through now.

To make the lemon filling, place the egg yolks in a medium-sized bowl.

In a large saucepan, mix the sugar and cornstarch, then slowly whisk in the water. Place the pan on the stove over medium heat. Stir constantly, and the mixture will begin to thicken, 4 to 5 minutes. Once the thickened mixture starts boiling, stir and cook for an additional 1 minute. This additional minute cooks out any cornstarch still remaining in the lemon filling.

(continued)

WHEN LiFE GiVES YOU LEMONS LEMON MERiNGUE PiE (CONT.)

Next, you will temper the egg yolks. "Tempering" is a fancy way of saying you heat up the egg yolks slightly before adding them directly into the filling. This way, the egg yolks don't scramble in the mixture.

Pour half of the thickened mixture into the egg yolks. Working very quickly, whisk the yolks and sugar mixture. When the egg yolks are completely incorporated, spoon the egg yolk mixture back into the saucepan full of the rest of the sugar mixture. Return the pot to the stove and stir over medium heat for an additional 2 minutes.

MERINGUE

5 egg whites (see egg-separating tips on page 10)

1 cup (200 g) granulated sugar

⅓ cup (80 ml) water

1 tsp vanilla

While on the heat, stir in the lemon zest, lemon juice and butter. Whisk constantly. Once the butter melts, remove the pan from the heat.

To make the meringue, place the egg whites in the bowl of a stand mixer fitted with a whisk attachment, and start mixing on low speed. Allow the egg whites to continue mixing on low speed while you begin the next step.

In a small saucepan, mix together the sugar and water and place over medium heat. When you place the pot over the heat, do not stir! Stirring the mixture may result in the formation of sugar crystals, which would force you to start over (we don't want a grainy meringue!). Without stirring, allow the sugar and water to come to 235 to 240°F (113 to 116°C), known as the soft-ball stage (see the Southern Caramel Cake recipe on page 42 for more information about this stage).

The tricky part about this recipe is timing the mixing of the egg whites with the sugar syrup. You want the egg whites to reach medium peaks by the time the sugar syrup has reached the soft-ball stage, which may require increasing the mixer speed depending on how long it takes for the sugar to heat up.

When the egg whites are at the medium peak stage and the sugar is at the soft-ball stage, adjust the mixer speed to medium and slowly stream the hot sugar syrup into the egg whites, which will begin to cook the egg whites. Be very careful when pouring because if you get splashed by the hot syrup, you may get burned. When all of the sugar syrup has been added, add the vanilla, then whip the egg whites for 5 to 8 minutes, or until the mixture has cooled down to room temperature.

To assemble the pie, spoon the tasty lemon filling into the blind-baked crust, spreading it evenly across the crust. Next, gently spoon the meringue onto the center of the pie. Very carefully, spread the meringue to the edges of the crust. The key is to have the meringue spread across the entire surface of the pie, touching the crust all the way around. I recommend using the back of the spoon to create little mini peaks on top of the pie. Just lightly tap the meringue. Place in the 350°F (175°C) oven and bake for 20 to 25 minutes in the middle of the oven, until the meringue turns golden brown. To ensure the egg whites are fully cooked, the internal temperature of the meringue should be 160°F (70°C).

Let the pie cool for 3 hours. Slice and serve. This lemony burst of flavor will definitely have people coming back for seconds.

ALL-AMERICAN APPLE PIE

Beloved all around America, the apple pie is famous for its flaky crust and flavorful filling. Though pies seem simple enough, looks can be deceiving. There is a lot that goes into making a pie from scratch, whether it be finding the right texture of the crust, making sure the filling isn't too watery or forming the perfect lattice design on top. But, with my instruction, you're going to nail it. In my pie crusts, I only use butter. While many bakers swear by vegetable shortening, I use butter because it gives the crust the best flavor, and I prefer the heartier effect from the dairy product as opposed to vegetable shortening.

YIELD: One 9-inch (23-cm) pie

DIFFICULTY: 🥄🥄

STANDARD PIE CRUST

2½ cups (315 g) all-purpose flour, plus more for rolling out the dough

1 tsp salt

1 tbsp (15 g) sugar

1 cup (227 g; 2 sticks) butter, very cold, cubed

4–8 tbsp (60–120 ml) very cold water

1 egg, lightly beaten

Get out a 9-inch (23-cm) pie dish and set it aside.

To make the crust, I live by the rule "prepare cold, bake hot." You will make the crust with freezing cold butter and cold water to develop the layers that make a crust flaky and tender.

Place the flour, salt and sugar in a food processor. Pulse a few times to evenly distribute the ingredients. Add the butter, and pulse for 1 minute. The mixture should resemble coarse sand, with small chunks of butter, almost resembling breadcrumbs.

Slowly stream in the water, 2 tablespoons (30 ml) at a time. You may not need the full amount specified in the ingredients list. The dough is ready when the flour-butter mixture starts sticking to itself and turns into a ball.

You can also do this process by hand in a large bowl, using a fork to incorporate the butter into the flour, then a spatula to stir in the cold water.

Dump the contents out onto your counter and slice in half. Form one-half into a disc, cover it in plastic wrap and stick it in the freezer. Lightly flour a surface, then roll the second disc of dough out into a circle using a rolling pin. The best way to do this is to roll in one direction, then rotate the dough and repeat until the dough is ¼ inch (6 mm) thick. Be sure to add more flour to your work surface so the dough doesn't stick to the counter.

(continued)

APPLE FILLING

½ cup (114 g; 1 stick) butter

3 tbsp (24 g) all-purpose flour

¼ cup (60 ml) water

1 cup (200 g) granulated sugar

2¼ lb (1 kg) apples (from about 7; I always use Granny Smith)

2 tsp (6 g) cinnamon

¼ tsp nutmeg

When the dough is the right thickness, you're ready to transfer it from the counter to the pie dish and this can be a bit scary. My favorite method is to wrap the dough around the rolling pin, hold the rolling pin over the pie dish, then unroll the dough. If all else fails, don't panic. One time my dough simply wouldn't stay together and I just grabbed the remains, dumped it into the pie dish, and used my hands to form an even layer of crust (I don't recommend this method!). Press your layer of dough flat into the pie dish, then trim off any excess around the edges, leaving only a small overhang of dough. Place the pie dish into the freezer while you make the filling.

To make the filling, start by preheating the oven to 425°F (220°C).

Add the butter to a saucepan, then place on medium heat on the stove. When the butter is fully melted, whisk in the flour, forming a paste. Stir constantly for 1 minute. Pour in the water and sugar, while constantly whisking, then cook the mixture until it starts to bubble vigorously, known as a rolling boil. Turn the heat to low but continue to simmer the mixture for an additional 2 to 3 minutes until the mixture thickens, then remove the pot from the heat.

Next, using a vegetable peeler, peel all the apples. Core the apples, meaning remove the core. If you don't have an apple corer, use a large knife to *carefully* slice each side of the apple off. Lay the apple sides flat-side down, then slice very thinly, about ¼ inch (6 mm) thick.

Place the apple slices in a large bowl, then pour in the cinnamon and nutmeg. Use a spoon to coat all of the apple slices with the spices. Then, pour the sauce over the apples. Stir to coat every apple slice with the sauce.

Remove the unrolled disc of pie dough from the freezer and let it soften slightly at room temperature until you are able to roll it out, about 5 minutes. Roll using the same technique as before, flouring the surface as you rotate the dough, to get a 9-inch (23-cm) circle that is ¼ inch (6 mm) thick.

Remove the pie dish with the dough from the freezer. Pour the apples coated in the sauce into the pie dough. If you'd like to play it safe, place the second half of the pie dough directly on top of the apples. (If you want to be fancy, see the Note for instructions for making a lattice.) Seal the dough at the edges of the crust by pressing down with a fork, then trimming off the excess dough with a pair of scissors. Using a knife, cut an "x" in the center of the pie. Using a beaten egg and a pastry brush (essentially a paint brush, but used for desserts), brush the egg all around the crust, coating everywhere. This technique will give the crust a beautiful shine when it comes out of the oven.

Bake the pie on a baking sheet at 425°F (220°C) for 15 minutes, then, while the pie is still in the oven, reduce the heat to 350°F (175°C) and bake for 45 minutes. Enjoy this classic, delicious pie warm out of the oven.

NOTE: Making a lattice on top is a bit tricky, so this technique goes out to my adventurous bakers! When you roll out the second layer of pie crust, use a pizza cutter or sharp knife to cut out seven ¾-inch (2-cm)-thick strips of dough. Place the first four strips of lattice on the pie. There should be some overhang; this will help us toward the end. Fold the first and third strips on top of themselves (the length of the dough strip should be half of its original size). Place one of the three remaining dough strips at the center of the pie, on top of the two strips of dough that weren't folded back. Unfold the layers we peeled back over themselves, then repeat this process with the second and fourth strips. You will see a woven pattern start to form. Rotate the pie dish and do this process one more time with the second and fourth lattice strips, forming a 4 x 3 woven pattern. Brush the lattice with the egg wash and bake as instructed above. If you're not up for the weaving challenge, lay the dough strips on top of each other, creating a grid rather than a weave.

SUMMERTiME PEACH PiE

Peaches are one of my absolute favorite fruits. I get so excited when they are in season, because they make for the perfect snack *and* vessel for a fantastic dessert. This pie delivers the warm, homey feeling you want in a dessert. It also happens to be a great recipe to practice technical skills in the kitchen, such as peeling and slicing fruit, preparing a pie crust and making a fruit filling.

YiELD: One 9-inch (23-cm) pie

DiFFiCULTY: 🥄🥄

2 lb (907 g) peaches

½ cup (100 g) brown sugar, lightly packed

¼ cup (50 g) granulated sugar

1 batch double-crust pie dough (see the All-American Apple Pie recipe on page 90)

3 tbsp (24 g) cornstarch

¼ tsp ground nutmeg

¼ tsp ground cinnamon

¼ tsp ground cloves

¼ tsp salt

2 tbsp (30 ml) lemon juice

1 tbsp (14 g) butter

1 egg, beaten

Begin by peeling the peaches. I find that blanching them allows the skin to peel right off, but any method of peeling the peaches will work. To blanch them, slice an "x" through the skin on the bottom of each peach, then place the peaches in a pot of boiling water for 45 seconds. Using a slotted spoon, transfer the peaches to a bowl filled with ice water. The skin should then peel off easily. After peeling, slice the peaches into ½-inch (1.3-cm)-thick slices, and place in a large bowl.

Sprinkle the brown and granulated sugars over the peaches, and set the bowl aside (at least 1 hour).

While the peaches sit, prepare half of the pie crust in a 9-inch (23-cm) pie dish as directed in the All-American Apple Pie recipe (page 90). Preheat the oven to 400°F (200°C).

After sitting for at least an hour, the peaches should have released a fair bit of juice. Drain the peaches through a sieve, saving the peach juice released by the sugar. Place the peaches back into the large bowl.

Place the peach juice in a saucepan with the cornstarch, nutmeg, cinnamon, cloves and salt.

Place on medium heat and stir constantly, getting rid of any clumps of cornstarch. Bring to a rolling boil, and once the mixture is boiling, cook for an extra 2 minutes.

Remove the thickened peach juice from the stove, then whisk in the lemon juice and butter. Pour that syrupy delight over the peaches and stir thoroughly, coating each peach.

(continued)

Place the peaches into your prepared pie crust and top with a lattice crust (see instructions in the Note of the All-American Apple Pie recipe on page 93). A lattice is a bit tricky, so this technique goes out to my adventurous bakers!

Brush the crust with the beaten egg and a pastry brush to create a beautiful golden shine on the crust when it is baked.

Place the pie dish on a baking sheet and bake for 50 to 55 minutes. Check the pie after 25 minutes. If it is browning too much, remove the baking dish, place a sheet of aluminum foil loosely on top, then continue baking.

Let the pie cool for a few hours, then slice and enjoy this incredible peach pie.

TOTALLY BANANAS! BANANA CREAM PiE

This past year, I've had a recent "obsession," if you will, with banana cream pie. I love the flavor of bananas and find that they work great in desserts. After extensive pie research, to my dismay, I found that many recipes take shortcuts by using instant pudding mixes and frozen "whipped topping." I 100 percent understand the appeal of these baking hacks, but if you have the time and ingredients, there is no reason not to make the perfect banana cream pie from scratch.

YiELD: One 9-inch (23-cm) pie

DiFFiCULTY: 🥄🥄

½ recipe pie crust (from the All-American Apple Pie recipe on page 90)

⅓ cup (41 g) all-purpose flour

¾ cup (150 g) granulated sugar

¼ tsp salt

3 egg yolks (see egg-separating tips on page 10)

3 cups (720 ml) whole milk

2 tsp (10 ml) vanilla extract

3 tbsp (42 g) butter

3 bananas

1 batch whipped cream (from The Secret Recipe Key Lime Pie recipe on page 85)

Preheat the oven to 375°F (190°C). Fill a 9-inch (23-cm) pie dish with the crust.

For this recipe, we do not need to bake the filling inside the pie crust, so we bake the crust prior to filling. This technique is called blind-baking. Using the same technique described in the *When Life Gives You Lemons* Lemon Meringue Pie recipe on page 87, blind-bake the crust for 25 to 30 minutes, until the edges and bottom are golden brown. While the crust is cooling, prepare the custard filling.

In a large saucepan, stir together the flour, sugar and salt. Set aside.

In a medium bowl, gently beat the egg yolks.

In a small saucepan, bring the milk to a boil over high heat. When the milk starts boiling, stir it into the saucepan with the flour mixture, little by little. Put the saucepan with the milk and flour over medium heat and bring the mixture to a rolling boil. This could take around 4 minutes. After the mixture starts to thicken, cook for an additional 1 to 2 minutes.

When the mixture has thickened, pour a small amount of it into the bowl of egg yolks. Immediately whisk the milk mixture into the egg yolks. This technique, known as tempering the eggs, introduces eggs to a certain amount of heat so that the yolks don't scramble when added back to the custard mixture. After you've incorporated a portion of the milk mixture into the egg yolks, pour this liquid back into the pot with the rest of the milk mixture. Return the pot to the stove on medium-high heat, constantly stirring. Cook for 1 minute longer.

Remove the pot from the heat, then add the vanilla and butter. Whisk to combine.

(continued)

TOTALLY BANANAS! BANANA CREAM PIE (CONT.)

Peel and slice the bananas on a cutting board, using a knife to cut the banana slices to an even thickness. The size of your banana slices is completely up to your preference, just make sure the slices are consistent. I prefer thinly sliced, so I can distribute the bananas all throughout the pie.

Sprinkle half of the banana slices on the bottom and sides of the prebaked crust. Top the bananas with the custard filling, then top the custard with the rest of the bananas, saving some for decoration.

Pour the whipped cream atop the luscious filling and form a dome shape with the cream and a rubber spatula. Top with a few slices of banana. I recommend refrigerating the pie for 2 hours before serving, and also serving the pie the same day you make it to make sure the bananas are fresh!

TRIPLE BERRY PIE

This triple berry pie is simply a classic. The balance of tart and sweet in the filling, along with the tender, flaky crust, is a great lesson on balancing flavors. You will make this pie and be amazed at your work. Adapted to be made quickly and easily, this recipe comes together effortlessly, as opposed to other pies in this book.

YiELD: One 9-inch (23-cm) pie

DiFFiCULTY: 🥄🥄

1 batch double-crust pie dough (see the All-American Apple Pie recipe on page 90)

2 cups (246 g) raspberries

2 cups (288 g) blackberries

2 cups (296 g) blueberries

⅓ cup (43 g) cornstarch

½ cup (100 g) granulated sugar

¼ cup (55 g) brown sugar

1 tbsp (15 ml) lemon juice

Zest of 1 lemon

½ tsp cinnamon

¼ tsp nutmeg

¼ tsp salt

1 egg, beaten

Preheat the oven to 400°F (200°C) and prepare half of the pie crust in a 9-inch (23-cm) pie dish (see the All-American Apple Pie recipe on page 90 for instructions).

To make the filling, combine the raspberries, blackberries, blueberries, cornstarch, granulated and brown sugars, lemon juice, lemon zest, cinnamon, nutmeg and salt in a large bowl. Lightly mix, being careful not to squash the berries.

Pour this mixture into the prepared bottom pie crust.

Roll out your top pie crust. This pie can be made using a lattice design on top (see instructions in the Note of the All-American Apple Pie recipe on page 93) or simply covering the pie with dough and cutting a slit in the center.

Many bakers talk about fluting the edge of a pie crust. This simply refers to crimping the edges or making an intricate design on the border of the pie. To make a traditional crimp, use both of your hands to hold a section of dough on the edge of the crust. The dough should be in between your index finger and thumb. Apply pressure from the thumb of your dominant hand, and once the indent has been made, shift your hands to the next segment of dough and repeat, using your thumb to make little "crimps" until the entire border of the pie looks beautiful! When I'm in a time pinch, I usually just press the edges of the crust down with a fork instead. Brush the top of the crust with the beaten egg. This step will give the crust an impeccable shine.

Bake the pie on a baking sheet for 45 to 50 minutes. Check on the pie after 25 minutes, and if the crust is browning too quickly, remove the pie, cover it loosely with a sheet of foil, then return the dish to the oven.

When done baking, allow the pie to cool on the counter for several hours to allow the filling to "set-up" or become firm and able to hold its shape.

Slice and serve!

GRANDPA'S FAVORITE CHERRY PIE

My grandparents on my dad's side, or as my family calls them, Grammy and Gramps, have inspired me to experiment with new flavors in the kitchen. For his 84th birthday, Gramps requested a cherry pie. I knew I had to make it extra special, so I made a classic cherry pie recipe "Matthew-style," meaning I used some flavors outside of the ordinary. As it turned out, my attempt was successful and both Grammy and Gramps said it was the best cherry pie they'd ever eaten—out of the many that they've tried over the past eight-plus decades.

YiELD: One 9-inch (23-cm) pie

DiFFiCULTY: 🍴🍴🍴

1 recipe double-crust pie dough (from All-American Apple Pie recipe, page 90)

4 cups (552 g) fresh cherries or 3 (14.5-oz [411-g]) cans sour cherries

1 cup (200 g) granulated sugar

⅓ cup (43 g) cornstarch

2 tbsp (28 g) butter

2 tbsp (30 ml) lemon juice

¼ tsp cinnamon

¼ tsp nutmeg

½ tsp vanilla extract

1 tsp balsamic vinegar (optional; see Note)

NOTE: Balsamic vinegar adds an acidity and depth of flavor that is uniquely delicious, but if you are looking for the classic cherry pie flavor, you may omit it.

Prepare the pie crust, following instructions in the All-American Apple Pie recipe on page 90. Preheat the oven to 400°F (200°C).

To make the filling, if you are using fresh cherries, pit all of the cherries. I recommend investing in a cherry pitter, but if you're like me and don't own one, the best way to go about this is to stand over the bowl of rinsed fresh cherries, slicing them in half, discarding the pits and placing the cherries into a large bowl. Yes, this is tedious but WOW it is worth the effort. Nothing compares to the freshness and love that goes into this process. You really can taste it. Stir in the sugar, cornstarch, butter, lemon juice, cinnamon, nutmeg, vanilla and balsamic vinegar (if using). The mixture is now ready to add to the prepared pie dish.

If you are using canned cherries, drain the liquid from the cherries into a separate bowl, then pour it into a saucepan, setting the cherries aside. Remove ¼ cup (60 ml) of the cherry juice from the pot and pour it into a small bowl. Whisk the cornstarch into the reserved cherry juice to form a slurry. Bring the cherry juice in the saucepan to a simmer over medium heat, then add the sugar. Continue to heat the juice until the sugar dissolves.

Add the cornstarch slurry into the sugar–cherry juice mixture. Stir continuously until the mixture is fully thickened, about 3 minutes. Then add the butter, lemon juice, cinnamon, nutmeg, vanilla and balsamic vinegar (if using). Stir the canned cherries into the thickened cherry filling, then let the mixture cool slightly.

Pour the cherry mixture into the prepared pie dish and form a lattice with the top crust (see instructions in the Note of the All-American Apple Pie recipe on page 93).

Bake the pie on a baking sheet for 40 to 45 minutes. At 25 minutes, check the crust and if it is browning quickly, place a sheet of foil loosely over the top of the pie and continue baking. Let the pie cool for at least 3 hours before serving. *Bon appétit!*

PERFECT PUMPKIN PiE

Everyone is in search of that perfect pumpkin pie, a staple of the fall season. From around Halloween to Thanksgiving, I think I'm always craving a slice of pumpkin pie. Pumpkin spice season just wouldn't be complete without making your very own pumpkin pie. The texture from homemade pumpkin pie is just so irresistibly good.

YiELD: One 9-inch (23-cm) pie

DiFFiCULTY: ♪♪

½ recipe pie crust (see the All-American Apple Pie recipe on page 90)

1 (8-oz [227-g]) package cream cheese, softened

1 (15-oz [425-g]) can pumpkin purée (not pumpkin pie filling!)

½ cup (114 g; 1 stick) butter, melted

1 tsp vanilla extract

3 eggs

3 cups (360 g) powdered sugar

1 tsp cinnamon

2 tsp (5 g) pumpkin pie spice (see Note)

¼ tsp salt

Whipped cream, for serving (optional)

NOTE: Pumpkin pie spice can be found in the spice aisle at the grocery store. To make it yourself, combine 1 tablespoon (8 g) of cinnamon, 1 teaspoon of ground cloves, ½ teaspoon of ground nutmeg and 1 teaspoon of ground ginger. Stir together, then measure out 2 teaspoons (5 g) for this recipe.

Prepare the pie crust (as directed in the All-American Apple Pie recipe on page 90), then preheat the oven to 400°F (200°C). Prebake the pie crust, following the blind-baking instructions on page 87 in the *When Life Gives You Lemons* Lemon Meringue Pie recipe, but for this recipe using a shorter prebaking time of 12 to 15 minutes, until the crust is a light, golden brown. This step is optional but I always prebake my pie crust when making pumpkin pie because the custard is so thick.

While the crust is prebaking, in the bowl of a stand mixer, or a large bowl if using a hand mixer, beat the softened cream cheese on high speed for 4 to 5 minutes. When it is light and creamy, pour in the pumpkin purée. Beat on medium speed for another 4 to 5 minutes.

Add the melted butter and vanilla extract, being sure to incorporate all the butter evenly.

Crack in the eggs, one at a time, mixing after each addition and scraping down the bowl with a spatula after each egg to ensure all of the ingredients are combined.

Finally, mix in the powdered sugar, cinnamon, pumpkin pie spice and salt.

Pour the pumpkin mixture into the prebaked pie crust, and carefully place the pie dish into the oven. Bake for 15 minutes at 400°F (200°C), then reduce the temperature to 350°F (175°C) and bake for 45 to 50 additional minutes. Check the crust after 25 minutes, and if it is browning too rapidly, remove the pie from the oven, cover the dish loosely with a sheet of aluminum foil, and continue to bake the pie as normal.

After you pull the pie out, let it cool in the refrigerator for a few hours, then you're ready to serve. Personally, I love my pumpkin pie with whipped cream.

MISSISSIPPI MUD PIE

I feel like Mississippi Mud Pie is one of those desserts that everyone has heard of but only a few people have tried. A few years ago, I don't think I even knew what a Mississippi Mud Pie was, besides that it had something to do with chocolate. It turns out that a Mississippi Mud Pie is a brownie baked on top of a crust with a chocolate custard on top . . . woah! This recipe is perfect for super special events, times when the dessert needs to be as over the top as the occasion. This dessert appears to be challenging because of the various different steps required, but I know with a little guidance you are going to be a Mississippi Mud Pie master.

YIELD: One 9-inch (23-cm) pie

DIFFICULTY: 🥄🥄🥄

CHOCOLATE COOKIE CRUST
25 chocolate sandwich cookies (such as Oreos®)

4 tbsp (56 g) butter, melted

BROWNIE FILLING
1¼ cups (284 g) unsalted butter

2 cups (440 g) light brown sugar

½ cup (100 g) granulated sugar

4 eggs

1½ cups (132 g) unsweetened cocoa powder

1 tsp salt

2 tsp (10 ml) vanilla extract

¾ cup (95 g) all-purpose flour

Get out a 9-inch (23-cm) springform pan.

To make the crust, place the whole cookies into a food processor (or crush the cookies by hand with a rolling pin in a ziptop bag if you don't have a food processor). Crush the cookies into fine crumbs, then pour in the butter. Blend for 20 more seconds, coating all the cookie crumbs.

Dump the cookie crumbs into the bottom of the springform pan and press firmly with your hands to pack the crust at the bottom of the pan. Set aside.

Preheat the oven to 350°F (175°C).

To make the brownie filling, in a small saucepan, heat approximately 2 cups (480 ml) of water until it boils, around 5 minutes. When the water is boiling, place a large, heat-safe bowl on top of the saucepan. The bowl should rest over the pot (the bottom of the bowl should not be touching the water). This method of cooking is called a double-boiler, or bain marie, which heats ingredients up without burning them. Place the butter and brown and granulated sugars into the large bowl and whisk constantly until the butter melts and the sugar fully dissolves, around 5 minutes.

Remove the bowl from the pot of boiling water and let it cool for 3 minutes. Whisk in each egg, one at a time. After adding all the eggs, whisk for an additional 5 minutes. This can be a bit of an arm-workout, and if you're not up for it, electric hand mixers work great here.

Then, whisk in the cocoa powder, salt and vanilla extract. Once combined, pour in the flour. Gently mix in the flour *just* until it is mixed in. Overmixing the flour could negatively affect the texture.

CHOCOLATE CUSTARD

1 batch chocolate filling (from As-Seen-on-TV Chocolate Cream Pie recipe on page 113)

1 batch whipped cream (from The Secret Recipe Key Lime Pie recipe on page 85)

Pour the brownie batter over the chocolate cookie crust, then bake for 45 to 55 minutes. To test if the brownie layer is done, insert a knife into the center and if it comes out clean, remove the pan from the oven.

While the brownie layer cools, prepare the chocolate custard as directed in the As-Seen-on-TV Chocolate Cream Pie recipe (page 113), but instead of pouring the filling into a pie dish, pour it into a bowl, then press a piece of plastic wrap onto the surface of the filling so a skin doesn't form on top. Chill until fully cooled. While the chocolate filling chills, make the whipped cream.

To assemble, pour the cold chocolate cream pie filling on top of the brownie layer, spreading evenly with a spatula. Then, spoon the whipped cream on top, and spread it into another even layer. Chill the entire pie for at least 2 hours, though I recommend overnight, covered with plastic wrap on top. Then unhinge the pie onto a serving tray. Slice and enjoy this decadent deliciousness.

BANOFFEE PiE

When I first learned that a dessert like Banoffee Pie existed, I was desperate to try it. For starters, the name "Banoffee" is a combination of "banana" and "toffee" . . . woah. Originating in the UK, this dessert is similar to a banana cream pie, but made with dulce de leche, adding a whole new depth of flavor. Though each component of a Banoffee Pie is relatively easy to make, preparing a proper dulce de leche sauce can be time consuming, but it is easy and so worth the time: The flavor is unmatched.

YiELD: One 8-inch (20-cm) pie

DiFFiCULTY: 🥄🥄

1 graham cracker crust recipe (from the Very-Berry Strawberry Cheesecake recipe on page 49; see Note)

1 (14-oz [396-g]) can sweetened condensed milk

2 bananas

1 batch whipped cream (from The Secret Recipe Key Lime Pie recipe on page 85)

1 bar of chocolate, for decoration (optional)

NOTE: In the UK, it is common to make the graham cracker crust with their equivalent of graham crackers, called "digestive biscuits." They are less sweet than graham crackers and can be found in the foreign aisle of many grocery stores. If you can't get your hands on some digestive biscuits, graham crackers will do the trick.

Press the graham cracker crust into an 8-inch (20-cm) tart pan with a removable bottom. If you don't own that piece of equipment, a pie dish will work, but the filling might not reach the top of the crust. Refrigerate the crust for 4 hours while you make the filling.

To make the dulce de leche, bring a large pot of water to a boil on the stove. This is where the recipe gets strange. Remove the wrapper from the sweetened condensed milk can, and then place the can—unopened!—into the pot of boiling water. Then, let it sit in the pot of boiling water for 3 hours, carefully turning it over every hour with tongs and adding water to the pot if a significant amount of water evaporates.

After boiling for 3 hours, let the can sit for 10 minutes before opening; the pressure created from boiling the can could lead to an explosion of sugary goodness. And just like magic, the once-white sweetened condensed milk will have turned into a beautiful golden dulce de leche.

Scoop this dulce de leche into the prepared graham cracker crust, and smooth it out. Cut the bananas into thin slices (the thickness is up to you, just keep the slices consistent in thickness). Sprinkle the bananas on top of the dulce de leche layer.

You can simply dump the whipped cream on the pie and spread it out, then serve, but if you want to be extra fancy, I recommend using a piping bag. See the Very Strawberry Cupcakes with Strawberry Frosting recipe on page 25 for piping tips. For this pie, I fit my piping bag with a large star tip, then make a ring of whipped cream around the border of the pie, just to make the presentation really pop.

To garnish, take a vegetable peeler and use the same motion as you would to peel a potato to "peel" a chocolate bar over the top of the tart. These mini chocolate curls will tie the entire dish together.

ABSOLUTELY NUTS! COCONUT CREAM PIE

Coconut Cream Pie is a classic dessert. Texturally, it is very similar to a Banana Cream Pie, yet gets a tropical feeling from the coconut. The texture of the custard filling paired with the light whipped cream and the flaky crust just create this absolutely delicious dessert. This recipe is one of my go-tos when I'm making desserts for friends.

YiELD: One 9-inch (23-cm) pie

DiFFiCULTY: 🥄🥄

½ recipe pie crust (from the All-American Apple Pie recipe on page 90)

1½ cups (360 ml) coconut milk (I use canned coconut milk!)

1½ cups (360 ml) half and half

5 egg yolks (see egg-separating tips on page 10)

¾ cup (150 g) sugar

4 tbsp (32 g) cornstarch

2 tbsp (28 g) butter

1 tsp vanilla extract

¼ tsp salt

1⅔ cups (155 g) flaked, sweetened coconut, plus ½ cup (47 g) for decoration (optional)

1 batch whipped cream (from The Secret Recipe Key Lime Pie recipe on page 85)

Preheat the oven to 375°F (190°C).

Prepare the pie crust in a 9-inch (23-cm) pie pan and blind-bake, following the directions in the *When Life Gives You Lemons* Lemon Meringue Pie recipe on page 87, for 25 to 30 minutes, until the edges and bottom are golden brown. While the crust is cooling, prepare the custard filling.

In a large bowl, whisk together the coconut milk, half and half and egg yolks. When the egg yolks are mixed in, set the bowl aside.

Pour the sugar and cornstarch into a medium saucepan over medium heat. Whisk together, and while whisking, slowly pour in the coconut milk mixture. Stirring constantly, allow the mixture to boil and thicken; this will take 4 to 6 minutes. When the mixture is thick and boiling, cook for an additional 1 minute.

Remove the pot from the heat, then whisk in the butter, vanilla, salt and flaked coconut.

Pour the warm custard into the prepared pie shell. Be sure to spread the custard evenly, using a spatula. Refrigerate the pie for 45 minutes to 1 hour to allow the coconut filling to become firm.

Spoon the whipped cream atop the chilled pie and spread evenly. I generally pile more whipped cream in the center of the pie to create the effect that the pie has a perfectly rounded top.

Optionally, I toast an extra ½ cup (47 g) of coconut by placing it into a pan over medium heat and constantly stirring until the coconut becomes golden brown, 3 to 6 minutes. The coconut will smell incredible. Once golden, remove the coconut from the heat and allow it to cool for 5 minutes. Then, sprinkle it atop the pie.

AS-SEEN-ON-TV CHOCOLATE CREAM PiE

This pie definitely has a unique backstory, stretching back to my time on Food Network's *Kids Baking Championship*. Arriving at the colossal TV studio kitchen for the first time, I was starting to feel a tinge of nervousness, though mostly still excited to have the opportunity. Once the first challenge was revealed to be a pie showdown, I knew I wanted to make a cream pie, as it would take less baking time than a berry pie, but still show off my 11-year-old baking skill set. I decided to go with my instinct and make a chocolate cream pie, because as a youngster (as I still am now), I go wild for all things chocolate. This pie is a symbol of a simple recipe with bright flavors that wowed the judges on the show, but was a dish I could make in the given time frame.

YiELD: One 9-inch (23-cm) pie

DiFFiCULTY: 🥄🥄

CRUST

½ recipe pie crust (from the All-American Apple Pie recipe on page 90)

CHOCOLATE FILLING

1⅔ cups (400 ml) water

3 tbsp (24 g) cornstarch

5½ tbsp (30 g) unsweetened cocoa powder

3 egg yolks (see egg-separating tips on page 10)

1 (14-oz [396-g]) can sweetened condensed milk

2 tbsp (28 g) butter

1 tsp vanilla

¼ tsp salt

TOPPINGS

1 batch whipped cream (from The Secret Recipe Key Lime Pie recipe on page 85)

1 bar of chocolate, for decoration (optional)

Preheat the oven to 350°F (175°C).

Prepare the pie crust in a 9-inch (23-cm) pie pan and blind-bake, following the directions in the *When Life Gives You Lemons* Lemon Meringue Pie recipe on page 87, for 25 to 30 minutes.

While the crust is blind-baking, make the custard. In a large bowl, whisk together the water, cornstarch and cocoa until no lumps remain. Stir in the egg yolks and sweetened condensed milk until the mixture is smooth. Pour the mixture into a medium saucepan, and turn the heat to medium, constantly stirring.

After 4 to 5 minutes, the mixture should start boiling and eventually thicken. When you notice the mixture becoming thick, cook for an additional 1 minute, being sure to stir very quickly.

When your delicious filling is done cooking, remove the pan from the heat, then stir in the butter, vanilla and salt. Let the filling cool slightly, around 10 minutes, then pour the filling into your prebaked pie crust. Cover the pie with plastic wrap and chill in the fridge while you prepare the whipped cream.

When the pie has chilled for 2 to 3 hours and is completely cold, top it with the whipped cream. I always pile the whipped cream in the center then use a rubber spatula to spread the whipped cream across the pie, creating a dome on top of the pie. Chill the pie again, for at least 1 hour or overnight for best results. This will ensure you get a nice clean slice when you cut the pie. If you'd like, shave a bar of chocolate with a vegetable peeler over the pie for a quick decoration.

MATTHEW-STYLE CARAMEL PECAN PiE

Now you're probably reading the title and wondering why I would call any dessert "Matthew-style," unless, of course, you've seen *Kids Baking Championship.* To make a long story short, the "unique" style and crazy flavor combinations I made on the show led to various baked goods that I made being dubbed "Matthew-style" by the judges. Ever since, the name really stuck and I look at it as a way to experiment and have fun in the kitchen. When I was really little, I have a vivid memory of my mom ordering a caramel pecan pie from a restaurant and me refusing to eat it because I was scared to try pecans. I ended up loving it, and this recipe pays homage to that funny memory.

YiELD: One 9-inch (23-cm) pie

DiFFiCULTY: 🖋🖋

½ recipe pie crust (from the All-American Apple Pie recipe on page 90)

36 soft caramel candies (the ones that come individually wrapped)

¼ cup (57 g; ½ stick) butter

¼ cup (60 ml) water

3 eggs

½ cup (100 g) granulated sugar

¼ cup (55 g) light brown sugar

2 tsp (10 ml) vanilla extract

¼ tsp salt

1⅓ cups (150 g) pecans (see Note)

1 egg, beaten (optional)

Ice cream, for serving (optional)

Preheat the oven to 350°F (175°C).

Prepare the pie crust as directed in the All-American Apple Pie recipe on page 90, and roll it into a 9-inch (23-cm) pie dish.

To make the filling, place the caramel candies, butter and water in a small saucepan and place on the stove over medium heat. Allow the caramels to melt completely. On my stove, this takes around 5 minutes.

Crack the eggs into a large bowl and add the granulated sugar, brown sugar, vanilla and salt. Using a whisk, beat the ingredients together until very well combined, 2 to 3 minutes. Pour the caramel mixture into the egg/sugar mixture and stir to combine.

Place the pecans on a cutting board, and using a large chef's knife, chop them into large chunks. If you have a food processor, feel free to pulse the pecans lightly. You don't want the pecan chunks to be too small. Mix the pecans into the egg and caramel bowl. Pour the mixture into the pie crust. I use a pastry brush to spread the beaten egg (optional) on the rim of the pie, which gives that exterior crust a gorgeous shine.

Bake on the middle rack of the oven for 35 to 40 minutes, or until the top is golden and has solidified. Remove the pie from the oven and give it a few hours to cool on the counter. I love serving this pie with vanilla ice cream!

NOTE: This step is optional, but I always scatter the pecans on a baking sheet and bake for 5 minutes at 375°F (190°C), just slightly toasting the nuts. This technique gives the pecans even more flavor.

CAMPFIRE S'MORES PIE

One thing I look forward to the most about summer is evenings sitting with friends by a campfire, roasting marshmallows. Great memories are made, but even better desserts are shared. A classic s'more roasted over a fire is honestly one of my favorite treats. This pie is my take on classic campfire s'mores—a graham cracker sandwich with a toasty marshmallow and milk chocolate—but in pie form.

YiELD: One 9-inch (23-cm) pie

DiFFiCULTY: 🥄

1 graham cracker crust (from the Very-Berry Strawberry Cheesecake recipe on page 49)

2 cups (12 oz; 340 g) semi-sweet chocolate chips

1 cup (240 ml) heavy whipping cream

4 cups (8 oz; 227 g) mini marshmallows (or 25 regular-sized marshmallows)

Preheat the oven to 350°F (175°C). Prepare the graham cracker crust according to the Very-Berry Strawberry Cheesecake recipe on page 49. Bake the crust for 8 minutes.

While the pie crust is baking, make the chocolate ganache. You may or may not have heard the term "ganache" thrown around in cooking terminology. I know it sounds super fancy and like some complicated dessert, but it's really just a type of chocolate sauce that's only two ingredients! When I found that out, it was a bit of a letdown to be honest . . . nonetheless, it is easy to make a ganache! Place the chocolate chips in a large bowl. It helps if the chocolate chips are at room temperature. Place the heavy cream into a medium saucepan and place over medium heat. Let the cream come to a simmer, but not a boil—your cream could spill out of the pot! Pour the hot cream over the chocolate chips. Let the chocolate and hot cream sit for 2 minutes, allowing the chocolate to melt. After 2 minutes, using a whisk, stir the mixture thoroughly until both ingredients fully blend to create a shiny liquid.

Pour the ganache into the graham cracker crust and refrigerate for 1 hour, or until the ganache is set, or firm.

If using full-sized marshmallows cut them in half (I find a pair of scissors works best for this). Sprinkle the marshmallows atop the ganache-filled pie crust and turn the oven on the broil setting. If your oven doesn't have this setting, use the hottest temperature.

Place the pie in the oven on the lowest rack, AND STAND BY THAT OVEN! This pie can go from golden to engulfed in flames in seconds. When the marshmallows have turned golden brown, around 5 minutes, immediately remove the pie from the oven.

Serve warm and enjoy this pie—it will make you feel like you are sitting by a warm, cozy campfire.

BLUE RiBBON BARS

Some of my favorite treats ever (*cough* blondies) are delicious, but don't really fit in a category of dessert. They aren't quite cookies, but they aren't quite cakes. Because each of these desserts are baked in one dish, then served squared, I resolved this baking dilemma by labeling them all as "bars."

As the chapter title says, these desserts are some of the best treats ever. These recipes are simple, yet never fail to impress. I think I make blondies at least once a week. The bars also happen to be perfect for bakers of all skill levels! Whether it be simple seven-layer bars or decadent brownies, there is something for everyone in this chapter.

THE BEST EVER BROWNIES

To be honest, I am a sucker for a box-mix brownie. The best part about using a mix is the crinkly-crispy top. So, when trying to achieve my favorite brownie recipe, I knew it had to have that crust on top. Made from scratch, these brownies are the best because the secret ingredient is love, which definitely isn't sold with the boxed mixes. Boxed mixes just don't give you the same authentic chocolate flavor and ultimate richness that making brownies from scratch provides.

YIELD: 12 brownies

DIFFICULTY: 🥄🥄

Cooking spray

¾ cup (95 g) all-purpose flour

¼ cup (22 g) unsweetened cocoa powder

½ tsp salt

½ cup (114 g; 1 stick) butter, cubed

1½ cups (252 g) semi-sweet chocolate chips, divided

¾ cup (150 g) granulated sugar

¼ cup (55 g) light brown sugar

2 eggs

1 egg yolk (see egg-separating tips on page 10)

2 tsp (10 ml) vanilla

Preheat the oven to 350°F (175°C). Cut a sheet of parchment paper into a square that fits into an 8 x 8–inch (20 x 20–cm) baking dish. Place the parchment paper in the baking dish and spray cooking spray on top of the paper and on the sides of the baking dish.

In a large bowl, whisk together the flour, cocoa powder and salt.

Place the butter and ½ cup (84 g) of the chocolate chips in a heat-safe bowl. Place 2 cups (480 ml) of water in a small saucepan and bring to a boil over high heat. Place the bowl of butter and chocolate on top of the pot of boiling water. The bowl should rest on top of the pot, but not touch the water. This technique is called a double-boiler, because we are heating the chocolate indirectly to avoid it seizing up or curdling. Stir constantly. When the chocolate has melted, remove from the heat and whisk in the granulated sugar and brown sugar. Whisk for 2 minutes. Then, mix in both eggs and the egg yolk, then the vanilla.

Add the flour-cocoa mixture into the chocolate mixture and gently stir in the dry ingredients, just until all the flour is incorporated. Last, stir the remaining 1 cup (168 g) of chocolate chips into the batter.

Pour the batter into the prepared dish and bake for 25 to 30 minutes, or until you can stick a toothpick in the center and it comes out with just a few crumbs on it. Cool for 1 hour, then slice into 12 pieces.

AWARD-WiNNiNG BLONDiES

YiELD: 12 to 15 blondies

DiFFiCULTY: ✒

In terms of desserts, I'm a simple guy. I love the classic flavor of a chocolate chip cookie and the texture of a fudgy brownie. This blondie recipe offers the best of both worlds; the brown sugar–vanilla flavor of cookies in brownie form. I didn't discover blondies until one summer when my cousins were having a baking competition for their swim team. Wanting to win, my cousins asked me to come over to their house and whip up the winning dessert. Upon arriving, I was shocked to see they had hardly any ingredients. With only 40 minutes until the competition, I was scrambling to come up with an idea, until I came across an old recipe for blondies. They were incredible and took first place! I was able to make them in a short amount of time with limited ingredients, showing how easy and simple these treats are to make.

Cooking spray

1½ cups (190 g) all-purpose flour

½ tsp baking powder

½ tsp salt

½ cup (114 g; 1 stick) butter, melted and cooled

1½ cups (330 g) brown sugar

2 eggs

2 tsp (10 ml) vanilla extract

1 cup (168 g) chocolate chips

Preheat the oven to 350°F (175°C) and spray a 9 x 9–inch (23 x 23–cm) baking dish generously with cooking spray.

In a medium bowl, whisk together the flour, baking powder and salt. Set aside.

In the bowl of a stand mixer (or a large bowl if using a hand mixer), mix the butter and brown sugar on high speed until the butter becomes light and fluffy, around 3 minutes.

Crack in the eggs, add the vanilla and mix until they are incorporated, about 1 minute. Scrape down the edges of the bowl with a rubber spatula.

Pour in the flour mixture and mix on low speed, just until all the flour is incorporated. Add the chocolate chips and mix on low speed for 1 to 2 minutes.

Pour the batter into the prepared baking dish, spreading it out with a spatula so the batter is in an even layer, and bake for 30 to 40 minutes, or until you can insert a toothpick into the center of the pan and it comes out clean.

You can slice the blondies while they are still warm and serve them out of the tray, or allow them to cool completely, flip the baking dish, remove the blondies, and slice into 12 to 15 squares and serve. Either way, you'll enjoy these delicious bars.

LUSCIOUS LEMON BARS

Lemon bars are just one of those desserts that I feel like society collectively does not talk about enough. They are basically a combination of cookies and lemon meringue pie. Balancing tartness and sweetness perfectly, lemon bars are just a fantastic dessert overall. The key is getting the texture right: The crust is not supposed to be super crispy or *too* soft. With a few pointers, you'll find that lemon bars are so simple, yet so delicious.

YiELD: Approximately 2 dozen bars

DiFFiCULTY: 🥄🥄

SHORTBREAD CRUST

2 cups + 2 tbsp (265 g) all-purpose flour

1 cup (120 g) powdered sugar

½ tsp salt

1 cup (227 g; 2 sticks) unsalted butter, melted

1 tsp vanilla

LEMON LAYER

2 cups (400 g) granulated sugar

¼ cup + 2 tbsp (47 g) all-purpose flour

6 eggs

1 cup (240 ml) freshly squeezed lemon juice

1 drop yellow food coloring (optional)

Powdered sugar, for decoration

Preheat the oven to 350°F (175°C). Line a 9 x 13–inch (23 x 33–cm) baking dish with parchment paper. It helps to have a little bit of extra paper hanging off the side of the dish so after baking you can remove the lemon bars with ease.

To make the crust, in a large bowl, whisk the flour, powdered sugar and salt together.

Stir in the melted butter and vanilla. Mix for around 3 minutes, until a dough forms.

Place the dough into the baking dish and, using your hands, press the dough into an even layer. Make sure to spread it into every corner: You want every lemon bar to have that tasty bit of crust!

Bake the crust for 15 to 20 minutes, just until the edges start to turn brown. Remove the pan from the oven and prick about 20 holes into the crust with a fork. This technique, known as docking the crust, helps the lemon filling stick to the crust.

While the crust is baking, make the lemon layer. Pour the sugar and flour into a large bowl. Whisk to combine the ingredients. Crack in the eggs and pour in the lemon juice and food coloring (if using, for a deeper yellow color). Stir with a whisk, just until the egg is incorporated. Pour the lemon mixture over the crust, then return the pan to the oven and bake for 20 to 22 minutes, until the center is fully set and does not jiggle.

Remove the pan from the oven. Cool at room temperature for 20 minutes, then put in the fridge for 1 hour.

Remove the lemon bars from the baking dish, dust with powdered sugar and then slice six to eight times vertically and three times horizontally.

DROP AND GIVE ME 7 (LAYER BARS)!

This is bootcamp after all, and no bootcamp is complete without small exercises to build up your strength. That's exactly what these 7-layer bars are: a way to practice some baking skills with a super simple recipe. The "7 layers" are simply layers of ingredients placed on top of each other. So instead of saying drop and give me 7 pushups, I'm saying drop and give me 7 . . . layer bars!

YiELD: 20 to 24 bars
DiFFiCULTY: 🥄

1½ cups (60 g) pretzels

¾ cup (170 g) butter, melted, plus 1 tbsp (14 g) butter, divided

1 lb (454 g) dark or semi-sweet chocolate chips (see Note), plus 1 cup (168 g) semi-sweet chocolate chips, divided

1 (14-oz [396-g]) can sweetened condensed milk

2 cups (4 oz; 114 g) mini marshmallows

1 cup (93 g) sweetened shredded coconut

1 cup (110 g) pecans, coarsely chopped

NOTE: If you like a sweeter bar, choose the semi-sweet chocolate, but the dark chocolate will give you a richer chocolate flavor.

Preheat the oven to 350°F (175°C) and grab a 9 x 13–inch (23 x 33–cm) baking dish.

Crush the pretzels in a food processor, or place them in a ziptop bag and crush them with a rolling pin. Add the pretzel crumbs to a medium bowl and pour in the melted butter. Mix to combine, then pour into the baking dish and press with your hands to form an even layer of pretzel crust.

Place the 1 pound (454 g) of chocolate chips in a microwave-safe bowl and add the sweetened condensed milk, then microwave for 1 minute. Stir, and if the chocolate is not completely melted, microwave in 30-second increments until the chocolate is completely melted and the mixture is smooth.

Pour the chocolate mixture evenly over the pretzel crust. On top of the chocolate, sprinkle the marshmallows, then the coconut, then the pecans.

Place the dish in the oven and bake for 25 to 30 minutes. This dessert will smell *so* good. Allow the bars to cool completely.

When the bars are cool, place the remaining chocolate chips in a microwave-safe bowl with the remaining 1 tablespoon (14 g) of butter. Microwave for 2 minutes, then stir. The chocolate should be nice and smooth.

Drizzle the chocolate over the cooled bars. I recommend spooning the chocolate into a sandwich bag, then cutting one of the bottom corners off the bag and adding the chocolate. This method really helps to create an "artistic" drizzle on top.

UNBELIEVABLE CARAMEL COOKIE BARS

These bars are dessert with a bit of family history. My grandma makes a variety of treats for the entire family around the holidays, and these caramel cookies are easily one of the most anticipated of the year. My grandma has been making the same recipe since she first immigrated to the United States! For years, she refused to share the recipe, but I've been given special permission to share it here. That's how you know these cookie bars are *extra* special.

YiELD: 24 bars
DiFFiCULTY: 🥄🥄

COOKIE CRUMBLE

2 cups (250 g) all-purpose flour

2 cups (160 g) quick-cook oats

1½ cups (330 g) brown sugar

1 tsp baking soda

½ tsp salt

1¼ cups (284 g) butter, softened

CARAMEL LAYER

14 oz (397 g) individually wrapped soft caramels (see Note)

⅓ cup (80 ml) milk

1 cup (168 g) semi-sweet chocolate chips

½ cup (55 g) pecans

NOTE: A variation of the recipe uses 1 cup (240 ml) + 3 tbsp (45 ml) caramel ice cream topping in place of the caramels.

Preheat the oven to 350°F (175°C) and grab a 9 x 13–inch (23 x 33–cm) baking dish. Place a large sheet of parchment paper inside the dish. It helps to have a bit of paper hanging off the sides of the dish to remove the bars easily after baking.

To make the cookie crumble, add the flour, oats, brown sugar, baking soda, salt and softened butter to the bowl of a stand mixer, or just a large bowl if making the bars by hand. Mix on low speed just until all the ingredients are combined, 1 to 2 minutes. The mixture should look crumbly.

Pour half of the cookie crumble part (approximately 3 cups [500 g]) into the baking dish. Press with your hands to form an even layer. Bake the bottom layer for 10 minutes. Set aside the rest of the cookie crumble mixture.

While the bottom layer is baking, place the caramels and milk in a microwave-safe bowl and microwave in 1-minute increments, stirring the mixture after every interval. It usually takes me 3 to 4 minutes in total to do this step.

Drizzle the warm caramel mixture over the warm crust. Spread the caramel in an even layer using a spatula or wooden spoon. Then, sprinkle the caramel with the chocolate chips and pecans.

Sprinkle the rest of the cookie crumble dough on top, covering the caramel layer. Bake for an additional 18 to 22 minutes, until the cookie crumb topping looks golden brown. Remove from the oven and allow to cool for 1 to 2 hours, then remove the bars and slice to your preferred size.

I hope you love these Caramel Cookie Bars as much as my family does.

PASTRY PARADISE

Bakers! Welcome to the pastry section of bootcamp! This chapter requires the most technique, skill and attention to detail but also contains some of the most delectable treats ever. Using techniques like making pastry cream, yeasted dough and more, you are sure to use these skills throughout your entire baking career. With the right pointers, making these recipes will turn you into a fantastic chef.

OOEY-GOOEY CiNNAMON ROLLS

Cinnamon rolls are certainly a labor of love. By the end of the process you have several dirty dishes and a messy counter, but most important, you will have a batch of warm swirls of sweet cinnamon goodness. Cinnamon rolls were the first advanced pastry I learned how to make, and they are a pastry you will love making, too.

YiELD: 12 cinnamon rolls

DiFFiCULTY: ✐ ✐ ✐

ROLLS

Cooking spray

1 cup (240 ml) milk

1 tbsp (12 g) active dry yeast

1 tbsp + ½ cup (115 g) granulated sugar, divided

2 eggs

6 tbsp (84 g) butter, melted

2 tsp (10 ml) vanilla extract

4¼ cups (530 g) all-purpose flour, plus more for rolling out the rolls

1 tsp salt

Spray a 9 x 13–inch (23 x 33–cm) baking pan with cooking spray. Set aside.

To make the rolls, add the milk to a microwave-safe bowl. Microwave for 30 seconds to 1 minute. We need the milk to be at a specific temperature. Yeast is actually a living organism (crazy, I know) that needs to be activated in a warm liquid. If the liquid is too hot, the yeast will die and your cinnamon rolls won't rise at all, but if the liquid is too cold, the yeast won't activate. The proper temperature for the warmed milk is 90 to 110°F (32 to 43°C). If you don't have a candy thermometer, a good way to test if the milk is the right temperature is to dip your finger in the milk. If the milk is warm, but not burning your finger, it is the right temperature.

Sprinkle the yeast and 1 tablespoon (15 g) of the sugar into the warm milk and lightly mix. Set the mixture aside for 10 minutes. In 10 minutes, the yeast mixture should be foaming. If this chemical reaction does not occur and no foam rises to the surface, it is possible your yeast didn't activate! If this is the case, start this step over again, making sure the milk is the correct temperature.

In the bowl of a stand mixer, crack in the eggs and pour in the butter, remaining ½ cup (100 g) of sugar and the vanilla. Pour in the activated yeast mixture and mix on medium speed until all the ingredients are combined. Add the flour and salt into the mixer (at this point you should use the dough-hook attachment). Mix until a dough comes together. Now, you need to knead the dough for 8 minutes. You can leave the mixer running using the dough hook at low speed for 8 minutes, or knead by hand (this takes some serious strength!) until the dough is smooth and elastic.

To test if your dough is done, try the windowpane test. Stretch a portion of the dough as thin as possible and hold it up to a window; if the dough is smooth and elastic, you should be able to see light from the window coming through the dough. If the dough is not done, it will tear rather than stretch thin and needs more kneading time.

(continued)

CINNAMON SWIRL

½ cup (114 g; 1 stick) butter, softened

1 cup (220 g) brown sugar, packed while measuring

2½ tbsp (20 g) cinnamon

CREAM CHEESE ICING

6 oz (170 g) cream cheese, softened

⅓ cup (75 g) butter, at room temperature

2 cups (240 g) powdered sugar

1 tsp vanilla extract

NOTE: A kitchen "life hack" is to use unflavored dental floss to slice your rolls. Take a long string of floss, wrap it around the roll and pull on both ends of the floss to slice through the dough. This is a great technique for beginners.

When the dough is ready, spray a large bowl with cooking spray and place the kneaded dough into the large bowl. Cover with a kitchen towel and let it rest for 1 hour. After an hour the dough should rise to double its size. Letting the dough rest so it can rise is called proofing the dough.

While the dough is rising, prepare the cinnamon filling. In a medium bowl, mix the butter, sugar and cinnamon. Stir until the sugar is incorporated into the butter. Set aside.

Once the dough has risen, "punch" or press on the dough to release any excess air, then lightly sprinkle flour on your counter so you can roll the dough without it sticking to the surface. Plop the dough onto the floured counter, and roll the dough out into a rectangle, approximately 14 x 9 inches (36 x 23 cm). Using a spatula, spread the cinnamon filling all over the dough in an even layer. Many chefs recommend leaving about 1 inch (3 cm) of space between the cinnamon sugar and the edges of the dough.

Roll the dough up very tightly, starting from the smaller side of the rectangle. When you've rolled the dough, flip the log upside down so the seam is facing down.

Slice the dough log into rolls using a serrated knife (a knife with ridges or teeth; or see the Note). Slice each roll 1 inch (3 cm) wide and discard the first slice, as it probably won't have a lot of cinnamon sugar.

Arrange the dough slices in the prepared baking dish. Cover the baking dish with a towel and let the cinnamon rolls rise for another hour.

While the dough rises for a second time, preheat the oven to 350°F (175°C) and whip up the cream cheese icing (you can also do this while the rolls are baking).

The icing is as simple as it gets! Add the cream cheese, butter, powdered sugar and vanilla to a medium bowl and stir together until an icing forms.

Bake the cinnamon rolls for 20 to 25 minutes, until beautifully golden on top. While the rolls are still warm, spread that delicious icing on top. I know I say a lot of desserts smell incredible out of the oven, but cinnamon rolls win by far for best smelling dessert. Enjoy your little masterpieces.

OOH LA LA ÉCLAIRS WITH CHOCOLATE GANACHE AND PASTRY CREAM

YIELD: 18 éclairs

DIFFICULTY: ✎ ✎ ✎

Éclairs are a notoriously challenging dessert. If you've never had an éclair, it is a hollow cylinder of baked dough filled with some sort of cream, topped with chocolate ganache. Technically, I'd say éclairs aren't as tricky as pretzels or cinnamon rolls but present a very specific set of challenges. First off, getting the éclair to puff up in the oven requires a lot of attention to detail. Making the pastry cream also requires focus, as not whisking enough can lead to a cream full of scrambled eggs. This French pastry *can* be mastered though, and éclairs are an absolutely fantastic dessert to eat.

ÉCLAIR SHELLS

½ cup (120 ml) water

½ cup (120 ml) milk

½ cup (114 g; 1 stick) butter

½ tsp salt

1 cup (125 g) all-purpose flour

4 eggs, plus 1 beaten egg, divided

Preheat the oven to 425°F (220°C). Line two large baking sheets with parchment paper.

To make the éclairs, add the water, milk, butter and salt to a saucepan. Place the pan over medium heat and stir until the butter melts. When the mixture reaches a simmer, or bubbles start to form on the sides of the saucepan, remove the mixture from the heat.

With the saucepan off the heat, stir in the flour. Really mix it in well until a paste forms. Move the saucepan *back* onto the stove over medium heat, and stir rapidly for 1 to 2 minutes, until the paste becomes smooth and forms a solid clump.

Dump the dough into the bowl of a stand mixer or large bowl if mixing by hand. Mix the dough on low speed until the mixture is no longer hot (it should be warm, but not burning hot), 5 to 6 minutes. You should see excess steam coming from the bowl while you mix.

Crack one egg into the batter and mix. The mixture will look curdled at first, but will start to come together. When the egg is fully incorporated into the dough, repeat until you've added the 4 eggs.

To form the éclairs, you will pipe the batter onto the prepared baking tray. To do this, add the dough to a piping bag fitted with a star tip (mine is ½ inch [1.3 cm]). See the Very Strawberry Cupcakes with Strawberry Frosting recipe on page 25 for tips on using a piping bag. If you don't have a piping bag, add the batter to a ziptop bag and snip off a small piece of one of the bottom corners.

(continued)

OOH LA LA ÉCLAIRS WITH CHOCOLATE GANACHE AND PASTRY CREAM (CONT.)

Apply pressure to the bag and squeeze to form a log of dough. My preferred éclair size is 4 inches (10 cm) long. Leave 1 to 2 inches (3 to 5 cm) of space between each log of dough. I usually use two baking sheets to space out the éclair dough, just to ensure they don't stick together.

I always brush my éclairs with a little bit of beaten egg on top, using a pastry brush. This step will give the éclairs a beautiful shine.

Bake at 425°F (220°C) for 10 minutes. After 10 minutes, reduce the oven temperature to 350°F (175°C), and bake for 30 minutes. It is super important to not open the oven while baking. Opening the oven will release the steam that puffs up the éclairs.

PASTRY CREAM

4 egg yolks (see egg-separating tips on page 10)

½ cup (100 g) granulated sugar

3 tbsp (24 g) cornstarch

¼ tsp salt

2 cups (480 ml) whole milk

1 tbsp (15 ml) vanilla extract

2 tbsp (28 g) butter

CHOCOLATE GANACHE

1 cup (168 g) semi-sweet chocolate chips

1 cup (240 ml) heavy whipping cream

When the éclairs are golden, remove them from the oven and allow them to cool while you are making the pastry cream. Add the egg yolks, sugar, cornstarch and salt to a large bowl. Whisk very rapidly, until the mixture turns pale yellow, around 1 to 2 minutes. Set aside.

Pour the milk into a large saucepan along with the vanilla. Bring the milk to a simmer, or until the milk at the edges of the pot starts bubbling. When the milk is simmering, you will temper the egg yolk mixture, meaning heat it up gently so that the yolks don't scramble when whisked into the pastry cream. Whisk the egg yolk mixture very quickly while simultaneously pouring in the hot milk (be sure to pour in the milk *very* slowly). When all of the milk has been added to the egg yolks, pour that entire mixture *back* into the saucepan.

Place the saucepan over medium heat and whisk the milk mixture constantly, until it begins to thicken, around 5 minutes. If you stop mixing, you risk the egg yolks scrambling in the pastry cream (yuck!). When the thickened pastry cream starts bubbling, whisk for 1 additional minute.

Remove the pastry cream from heat and stir in the butter. When the butter has melted, I always push the hot cream through a sieve into a clean bowl to remove any lumps. This step is optional, but I'd recommend it. Top the pastry cream with a sheet of plastic wrap that touches the cream (this prevents a layer of dryness from forming on top of the cream). Refrigerate until chilled, 1 to 2 hours.

To make the ganache, place the chocolate chips into a large bowl. Pour the heavy whipping cream into a microwave-safe bowl and microwave for 1 minute, 30 seconds. Pour the hot cream over the chocolate chips and let the bowl sit for 1 minute. Whisk the chocolate chips and cream together. If the chocolate isn't fully melted, microwave the ganache in 30-second increments, stirring after each one, until the ganache is smooth. See, a ganache is much simpler than the name makes it out to be!

Assembling the éclairs is easier than it might seem. Some people inject their éclairs with pastry cream, but I slice my éclairs open like a hotdog bun, then pipe the pastry cream in.

To assemble, dip the top of the éclair shell into the ganache, then carefully cut it open lengthwise. Place the pastry cream into a piping bag with a star tip (see the Very Strawberry Cupcakes with Strawberry Frosting recipe on page 25 for piping hacks). Pipe the cream onto the bottom layer of the éclair, then top with the ganache-coated half.

There you have homemade éclairs!

BETTER-THAN-MALL SOFT PRETZELS

My favorite part of going to the mall is definitely getting a soft pretzel. They are one of those treats that you only indulge in every once in a while, but taste incredible every time. Besides buying pretzels at the mall, I have other fond memories of making my own soft pretzels. After being on *Kids Baking Championship*, I was fortunate enough to make a guest appearance on co-host Valerie Bertinelli's Food Network show, *Valerie's Home Cooking*, where we prepared soft pretzels. Filmed in the hills of Hollywood, I received "the star treatment," seeing how the production team renovated a real house into a TV studio. I remember being so happy that day, so I am attempting to share that joy I felt through these tasty pretzels. We'll be perfecting a yeasted dough, along with learning about how pretzels get that delicious brown color (spoiler alert, it's from baking soda!).

YiELD: 12 pretzels

DiFFiCULTY: 🥄 🥄 🥄

PRETZEL DOUGH

1¼ cups (300 ml) water

1 tbsp (12 g) active dry yeast

1 tbsp + ½ cup (115 g) granulated sugar, divided

4½–5 cups (560–625 g) all-purpose flour

1½ tsp (9 g) salt, plus coarse salt for decoration (optional)

1 tbsp (15 ml) vegetable oil

Cooking spray

½ cup (114 g; 1 stick) butter, melted, for serving

To make the pretzels, pour the water into a microwave-safe bowl. Place in the microwave for 30 seconds. It should be warm, but not hot. See the Ooey-Gooey Cinnamon Rolls recipe on page 132 for tips on the correct temperature and other tips for activating yeast. Sprinkle the yeast and 1 tablespoon (15 g) of the sugar into the warm water and let the bowl rest for 10 minutes.

In the bowl of a stand mixer, mix 4½ cups (560 g) of the flour with the salt. When the yeast has activated and is foamy, pour it into the bowl of the stand mixer, along with the oil. Mix using a dough hook until the dough comes together. If the dough is too sticky to handle, add more flour, little by little, up to 5 cups (625 g).

Now, you need to knead the dough for 8 minutes. You can do this step by hand, folding the dough over itself on a floured surface for 8 minutes, but you'd need some big muscles for that. I recommend turning your mixer on low speed and letting the dough be worked by the dough hook attachment for 8 minutes, until the dough is smooth and elastic. See the Ooey-Gooey Cinnamon Roll recipe on page 132 for a way to test if your dough is ready.

When the dough is kneaded, spray a large bowl with cooking spray and plop the ball of dough into the bowl. Cover the bowl with a kitchen towel and place it in a warm spot to proof, meaning rise for 1 hour. I recommend placing your oven on the lowest heat setting with the door cracked open as a place for the dough to proof.

(continued)

BAKING SODA DIP

4 cups (960 ml) water

½ cup (110 g) baking soda

After 1 hour, the dough should be doubled in size. If it has doubled, "punch" it down, or press on it to remove the excess air. Lightly sprinkle flour on a countertop, then plop the dough onto the counter and cut it into twelve equal pieces. Try not to handle the dough more than you need to, because the more you handle the dough, the more difficult it is to work with.

Working with one chunk of dough at a time, roll each chunk into a long rope. The longer the rope, the easier the dough will be to form into a pretzel.

To shape the pretzels, first make the rope of dough into a "U" shape. Next, fold the top two corners over each other (bring the upper right corner of dough toward the lower left and the upper left side of the dough to the lower right area). When the strands of dough are crossing over each other, twist them around each other, creating the twist in the center of the pretzel, and pull the strands to the bottom of the U shape, thus creating a pretzel. There are tons of informative videos online going in-depth on shaping pretzels.

At this point, preheat the oven to 450°F (230°C).

While the oven is preheating, make the baking soda dip. In a saucepan, bring the water to a boil. Stir in the baking soda. Immediately pour this mixture into a shallow baking dish, or other container big enough to dip the pretzels in. This baking soda solution will give the pretzels their iconic flavor. Allow the baking soda solution to cool for about 5 minutes, or until you can comfortably dip your hand in it. Dip the pretzels into the baking soda solution. This step is the most difficult in the process, and it may be difficult to keep your pretzel together. Being gentle will help. After dipping the pretzel dough, immediately transfer it to a baking sheet. Repeat this process until you run out of pretzels. Sprinkle the tops of the dough with coarse salt, if you'd like, then bake for 8 minutes, or until the pretzels are nice and brown on top.

Finish the pretzels by brushing them with melted butter.

GOURMET POP TARTS

One of the most famous American snacks, Pop Tarts® are wildly popular. The concept of a Pop Tart is just so ingenious that it's begging to be remade as a gourmet treat. Using real pie crust, fresh jam and homemade icing, our Pop Tarts are a gourmet take on the classic (and a better version, in my humble opinion. . .).

YiELD: 6 pastries
DiFFiCULTY: 🥄🥄

STRAWBERRY JAM

1 lb (454 g) fresh strawberries

1½ cups (300 g) granulated sugar

2 tbsp (30 ml) lemon juice

1 tbsp (6 g) lemon zest

CRUST

1 recipe pie crust (from the All-American Apple Pie recipe on page 90)

Flour, for rolling out the dough

Chop the stem off of each strawberry, and cut them into fourths. Add the strawberries to a saucepan with the sugar, and stir continuously over medium heat. As the strawberries heat up, they will break down and become syrupy. Once the strawberries begin to boil, add the lemon juice and zest.

Let the mixture boil for approximately 15 more minutes (until it reaches 220°F [105°C] if you have a candy thermometer). Pour the jam into a heat-safe bowl and refrigerate until chilled.

While the jam is chilling, prepare the pie dough. Form the dough into two discs, then wrap in plastic wrap and chill for 30 minutes.

When the dough is chilled, sprinkle a counter with flour, then roll out one disc of the pie dough into an approximately 11 x 13–inch (28 x 33–cm) rectangle. Because you will need sharp edges for your Pop Tarts, use a knife to trim the edges to get a 10 x 12–inch (25 x 30–cm) rectangle. Cut a line horizontally through the middle of the dough, then make three even vertical cuts, giving you six rectangles.

Repeat this process with the second disc of dough.

Line two baking sheets with parchment paper, then arrange three rectangles of dough on each sheet. Dollop 2 tablespoons (30 ml) of jam in the center of each rectangle and spread it out slightly, but not all the way to the edges. You need a clean border so the dough layers will stick together and the jam won't seep out. Top with another layer of dough on each rectangle. Use a fork to seal the edges, by pressing down on each of the seams. Freeze the trays for 1 hour.

(continued)

GOURMET POP TARTS (CONT.)

ICING

2 cups (240 g) powdered sugar

2–3 tbsp (30–45 ml) milk

½ tsp vanilla extract

Sprinkles, for decoration (optional)

Place the frozen Pop Tarts in the oven and bake for 25 to 30 minutes, or until the tarts are golden brown. Allow the pastries to cool before icing.

While the Pop Tarts are baking, make the icing. In a large bowl combine the powdered sugar, milk and vanilla. Whisk until an icing forms. Start with 2 tablespoons (30 ml) of milk, and if you'd like the frosting thinner, add more milk, 1 tablespoon (15 ml) at a time.

Dip the pastries into the icing, or spread the icing on top of each pastry. Top with sprinkles if you'd like and enjoy your homemade version of an American classic.

THE BEST BRiOCHE BREAD

I first discovered how incredible it is to make fresh brioche bread during the beginning of the COVID-19 2020 shutdowns. Locked inside, I wanted to expand my bread-making horizons, and I *knew* I needed to make brioche. If you're unfamiliar with brioche, first off, you're missing out. It's this incredibly soft bread that almost tastes like cake. Ever heard the expression "Let them eat cake?" The translation from French actually translates to "Let them eat brioche." In short, this bread is fit for a king.

YiELD: One loaf

DiFFiCULTY: 🥄🥄🥄

SPONGE

½ cup (120 ml) warm milk

1 packet (2¼ tsp; 9 g) active dry yeast

1 tbsp (15 g) sugar

1 cup (125 g) all-purpose flour

DOUGH

6 eggs

3 cups (375 g) all-purpose flour, plus more for rolling out the dough

½ cup (100 g) granulated sugar

2 tsp (12 g) salt

1 cup (227 g; 2 sticks) butter, softened

Cooking spray

1 egg, beaten

You are going to make brioche in two parts; you will start by making a paste with a base of flour and yeast known as a "sponge" in bread-making terms. It will give the bread a super fluffy texture. Start by heating the milk. See the Ooey-Gooey Cinnamon Rolls recipe on page 132 for instructions on heating the milk.

To the bowl of a stand mixer, add the warm milk, then the yeast, then the sugar and flour. Mix the ingredients using a spatula, until a paste forms, 1 to 2 minutes. Cover the bowl with a kitchen towel and allow the sponge to sit at room temperature for 1 hour. After 1 hour, the sponge should have developed lots of little bubbles, proving that the yeast was activated. If this hasn't happened, restart this step, making sure the milk is the correct temperature.

When the sponge has formed, it's time to make the dough. Add the eggs, flour, granulated sugar and salt. Mix using the dough hook on your mixer, on low speed. Be sure to scrape down the edges of the bowl with a spatula to ensure all of the ingredients are evenly combined. When they are well combined, turn the mixer up to medium-high speed and mix the dough for a solid 5 minutes, or until the dough passes the windowpane test (see the Ooey-Gooey Cinnamon Rolls recipe on page 132).

After 5 minutes, add the butter, 2 tablespoons (28 g) at a time. Wait until the butter is completely incorporated before adding the next 2 tablespoons (28 g). Repeat this process until you are out of butter. When all of the butter is incorporated, knead the dough (meaning, keep mixing it) for 4 minutes.

(continued)

Coat a large bowl with cooking spray and place the brioche dough (which should be shiny and stretchy) into the bowl. Cover the bowl with plastic wrap and set it aside for 1 hour. Within 1 hour, the dough should have risen to double its original size. It may take longer than an hour for this process.

When the dough has risen, sprinkle flour on a counter and dump the dough on the floured surface (it will be sticky!). Cut it into six equal-sized chunks of dough. I find that using a pair of scissors is helpful to separate the dough.

You will now form each chunk of dough into a "roll." To do this step, flatten each chunk of dough into a rectangle. Fold the dough like a business letter, meaning fold the short ends of the rectangle into the center. Flip the dough 90 degrees and roll it into a log, starting from the short end. Make the log as tight as possible.

After rolling each dough piece into a log, generously coat a 5 x 8-inch (13 x 20-cm) loaf pan with cooking spray.

Squeeze the six dough logs into the loaf pan. Cover the pan with plastic wrap and let the dough rise for an additional 1 hour, or until the dough is fully doubled in size again (I know this process seems tedious, but it's so worth it).

While the dough rises, preheat the oven to 375°F (190°C). Generously brush the risen bread dough with the beaten egg (I use a pastry brush). The egg is going to give the bread a shiny, golden crust.

Bake the loaf for 30 minutes, or until it turns a beautiful golden-brown color. Let the loaf cool for 10 minutes at room temperature, then remove the brioche from the loaf pan. Allow the loaf to cool completely, then slice.

COZY APPLE STRUDEL WITH CARAMEL SAUCE

YIELD: 8 servings

DIFFICULTY: 🥄🥄🥄

Authentic apple strudel is one of the most delicious desserts ever invented, and it has roots in Austria. The recipe I am sharing with you is close to an Austrian strudel, but we are not making the dough from scratch. Spending the entire day making the dough, stretching it paper thin, and having hundreds of variables to stress about in the kitchen makes me sway in the direction of using phyllo dough, a delicious alternative. Using phyllo dough is a great introduction to apple strudel and will make for a deliciously crisp recipe.

APPLE STRUDEL

1 (1-lb [454-g]) package frozen of phyllo dough

⅓ cup (48 g) raisins

2 tbsp (30 ml) water

½ cup (114 g; 1 stick) unsalted butter

1½ lb (680 g) apples (I use Granny Smith)

3 tbsp (42 g) brown sugar

1 tbsp (15 ml) lemon juice

Zest of 1 lemon

½ tsp cinnamon

¼ tsp salt

3 tbsp (45 g) granulated sugar

⅓ cup (18 g) panko breadcrumbs

Powdered sugar, for serving

To make the strudel, if your phyllo dough is frozen, place the box in the fridge overnight to thaw.

Preheat the oven to 350°F (175°C).

To begin, prepare the raisins. Personally, I hate raisins, but they are traditionally found in apple strudel and I feel like I'd be doing you a disservice to omit them from the recipe! Place the raisins and water in a microwave-safe bowl and microwave for 20 seconds. This process will make the raisins softer and easier to eat within the strudel. Drain the water from the raisins and set aside.

Melt the butter. I do this in a microwave-safe bowl, microwaving in 30-second increments until the butter is melted. Set aside.

Peel the apples. Slice the apples into quarters, then slice the apple pieces into strips. Then rotate the strips 90 degrees, and slice the strips into cubes. Combine the apples with the brown sugar, raisins, lemon juice, lemon zest, cinnamon and salt in a large bowl and set aside.

Unroll your phyllo dough from the packaging and remove six sheets. Be very gentle because phyllo dough is very thin and rips easily. Place a moist kitchen towel over the sheets of phyllo, or else they will dry out. Refreeze the unused phyllo sheets.

(continued)

CARAMEL SAUCE

1 cup (200 g) granulated sugar

6 tbsp (84 g) butter, cubed and softened

½ cup (120 ml) heavy cream

1 tsp salt

Tear off a large piece of parchment paper, larger than the phyllo rectangles, to assemble the strudel. Place one layer of the phyllo dough on the parchment paper, then brush the phyllo with some of the melted butter. Sprinkle a teaspoon of the granulated sugar on top of the buttered phyllo. Top with the next layer of phyllo dough and repeat until you run out of dough layers (don't brush butter on the top layer).

Pour the breadcrumbs in a rectangle within the phyllo dough sheet, about 3 inches (8 cm) in width. You want to leave 2 inches (5 cm) of space between the breadcrumbs and the edges of the dough.

Spoon the apple mixture over the breadcrumbs. I use a slotted spoon to transfer the apples. This gets rid of excess liquid.

Now, you will use the parchment paper to help roll the strudel. If you've ever rolled a burrito, it is a similar technique. Roll the long edges of the phyllo dough rectangle to the center, then going from the short end, roll the entire sheet into a log. Place the seam side down on the parchment paper. Transfer the apple log (on the parchment paper) to a baking sheet. Brush the top of the dough with more butter and sprinkle on the remaining granulated sugar. Bake for 45 to 55 minutes, until the dough is golden brown.

While the strudel is baking, make the caramel sauce. Place the sugar in a medium saucepan over medium heat. Using a heat-proof spatula, stir the sugar as it slowly starts to melt into a syrup. The sugar will start to form clumps, then melt into a deep amber syrup.

When all of the clumps of sugar have fully melted, add the butter. I highly recommend you use softened butter because as soon as you add the butter, it will start bubbling vigorously, and using cold butter may cause hot sugar to splash on you. Whisk the butter rapidly into the sugar. When combined, pour in the heavy cream and stir until a caramel sauce forms. Pour the sauce into a heat-proof bowl, then stir in the salt.

Drizzle the warm caramel over the toasty apple strudel. Cut the strudel into 1-inch (3-cm) slices. I always tap a bit of powdered sugar through a sieve for an easy, elegant garnish.

VERY-BERRY STRAWBERRY SHORTCAKE

YiELD: 12 shortcakes

DiFFiCULTY: 🥄🥄

This strawberry shortcake recipe is near and dear to my heart. Inspired by the recipe I made the most from the first cookbook I owned, I wanted to include a similar recipe in the first cookbook I wrote. Strawberry shortcakes are a light dessert that take me back to the summer. Essentially, a strawberry shortcake is a biscuit served with whipped cream and strawberries. Its simplicity is the very factor that makes this dessert so tasty.

BISCUITS

4 cups (500 g) all-purpose flour, plus more for rolling out the dough

2 tbsp (28 g) baking powder

2 tbsp (30 g) granulated sugar

2 tsp (12 g) salt

¾ cup (170 g; 1½ sticks) butter, cold, cubed (see Note)

¾ cup (180 ml) buttermilk or whole milk

1 egg, beaten

WHIPPED CREAM

1 cup (240 ml) heavy cream

2 tbsp (16 g) powdered sugar

1 tsp vanilla extract

STRAWBERRIES

6–7 cups (864 g–1 kg) strawberries

2 tbsp (28 g) brown sugar

1 tbsp (15 g) granulated sugar

1 tbsp (15 ml) lemon juice

Preheat the oven to 425°F (220°C) and fully cover a baking sheet with a piece of parchment paper.

To make the biscuits, add the flour, baking powder, sugar and salt to a food processor. Pulse for a few seconds to distribute the ingredients.

Add the very cold butter to the food processor and pulse until the mixture resembles coarse crumbs. The butter should be in small chunks, around the size of a pea. Pour in the buttermilk and blend until a solid dough forms.

Sprinkle some flour on the counter, and carefully transfer the dough from the food processor onto the floured surface. Pat the dough into a rectangle, approximately 1 inch (3 cm) thick. Fold the dough in half, then repeat this process. The final rectangle should be 6 x 10 inches (15 x 25 cm). Cut 3-inch (8-cm) circles out of the dough. If you don't have a cookie cutter, you can use a drinking glass.

Arrange the biscuits on the parchment-lined baking sheet (it's alright if they stick together) and brush the tops with the beaten egg.

Bake for 10 to 15 minutes, or until the tops of the biscuits are beautifully golden brown. Remove the biscuits from the oven and let them cool on the baking sheet.

While the biscuits cool, prepare the whipped cream. Place the heavy cream, powdered sugar and vanilla extract in the bowl of a stand mixer and whip on medium speed until the cream becomes aerated and stiff, 3 to 4 minutes.

To prepare the strawberries, chop the stems off the strawberries. Slice the berries thinly. I always slice vertically, but you can slice your strawberries to your preference.

Place the berries in a large bowl with the brown and granulated sugars and the lemon juice. Let the mixture sit for 5 to 10 minutes in the fridge before serving. The strawberries will release their juices and mix with the sugars to create a syrup. That process is called macerating the berries.

To assemble the strawberry shortcakes, split each biscuit in half and spoon a generous amount of whipped cream on top, then top with strawberries. If you want more whipped cream and strawberries, feel free to spread whipped cream and strawberries on the top of the biscuit as well.

NOTE: I recommend popping the butter into the freezer for a few minutes before preparing the biscuits.

DONUT DEPOT

Donuts are one of the most beloved desserts of all time, so I devoted an entire chapter to giving my favorite tips so that you can make your very own donuts from home. Making dough with yeast can certainly be intimidating, but it is nothing out of your skill set. Just in case you wanted a few "warm-ups" before jumping into the classics, I included a few cake donut recipes ;). My best tip for making donuts with yeast is to ensure the yeast is fully activated before continuing with the recipe. When activating your yeast, the water/milk temperature should be around 110°F (43°C), called lukewarm. If your yeast doesn't create a foam at the top of the liquid, I would recommend trying again with new ingredients. Also, be sure to knead the dough until it is fully smooth. Not kneading my dough enough was a mistake I made a little too often growing up. With some good ol' fashioned hard work, I know you can make fantastic, fresh donuts. This is your personal depot of donuts.

VANILLA CAKE DONUTS

While making yeasted donuts (you know, the ones that take multiple hours?) is a great test of some tricky baking techniques, sometimes you just want a donut without all the fuss. Plus, frying donuts at home for the first time can be intimidating. These cake donuts are baked rather than fried, and a tasty treat that is not quite as big of a challenge as traditional donuts.

YIELD: 6 donuts

DIFFICULTY: ✐

DONUTS

Cooking spray

1 cup (125 g) all-purpose flour

⅓ cup + 2 tbsp (96 g) granulated sugar

1 tsp baking powder

½ tsp nutmeg (optional)

¼ tsp salt

2 tbsp (28 g) butter, melted

1 egg

⅓ cup + 2 tbsp (110 ml) milk

2 tsp (10 ml) vanilla

VANILLA DONUT FROSTING

1 cup (120 g) powdered sugar

2 tbsp (30 ml) milk

1 tbsp (14 g) butter, melted

½ tsp vanilla extract

Sprinkles, for decoration (optional)

Preheat the oven to 350°F (175°C) and spray a donut pan with cooking spray. If you don't have a donut pan, you can also use a muffin tin (just spray each hole!).

In a large bowl, whisk together the flour, sugar, baking powder, nutmeg (if using) and salt. Set aside.

In a medium bowl, whisk together the melted butter, egg, milk and vanilla.

Pour the milk mixture into the dry ingredients. Stir using a wooden spoon or rubber spatula. When all the flour is incorporated into the batter, you are ready to bake!

Fill each donut cavity three-quarters full of batter. When you've filled the entire donut pan or muffin tin, bake the tray for 8 to 10 minutes, or until you can insert a toothpick into the center of a donut and it comes out clean.

Let the donuts cool for 10 to 15 minutes, then run a knife around the sides of each one and flip the tray over to pop out your fluffy donuts.

To make the glaze, whisk the powdered sugar, milk, melted butter and vanilla in a bowl for around 1 minute. You should have a beautiful glaze!

Dip the round side of the donuts in the glaze. The donuts are a bit delicate, so be gentle! Finish by adding sprinkles on top, if desired. Boom: simple, easy donuts.

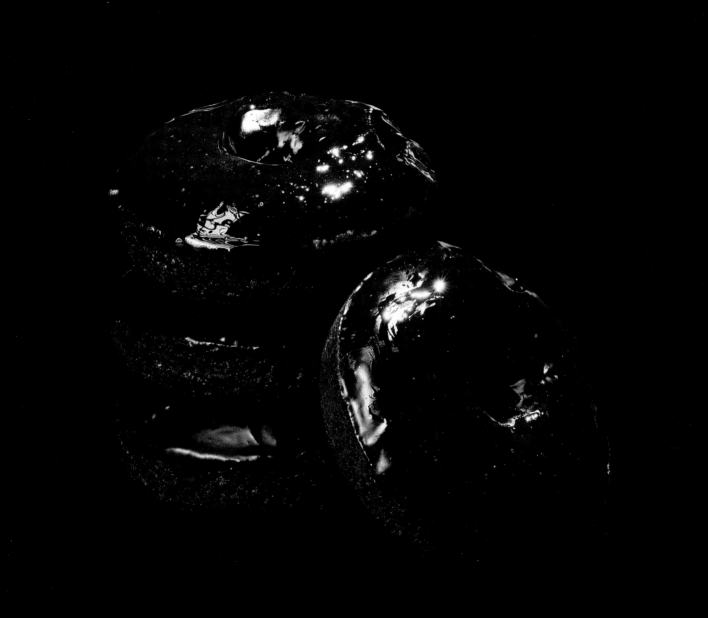

CHOCOLATE CAKE DONUTS

I love baking my own version of desserts I would normally buy. It's a great way to challenge myself in the kitchen, knowing how I want the dessert to turn out. When I go to a donut shop, if I'm getting a donut, I'll choose a chocolate cake donut. I love the texture (and the chocolate, duh!). These simple, easy and quick chocolate donuts are a great dish for kitchen beginners!

YiELD: 8 donuts
DiFFiCULTY: 🥄

CHOCOLATE DONUTS

Cooking spray

1 cup (125 g) all-purpose flour

¼ cup (22 g) unsweetened cocoa powder

½ cup (100 g) granulated sugar

½ tsp baking powder

½ tsp baking soda

¼ tsp salt

1 egg

⅓ cup (80 ml) milk

¼ cup (60 ml) sour cream

2 tbsp (28 g) butter, melted

1 tsp vanilla extract

CHOCOLATE GANACHE GLAZE

½ cup (84 g) semi-sweet chocolate chips

½ cup (120 ml) heavy whipping cream

Sprinkles, for decoration (optional)

Preheat the oven to 350°F (175°C) and generously spray a donut tray with cooking spray, or if you don't have a donut tray, spray a muffin tin with cooking spray.

To make the donuts, in a large bowl, whisk together the flour, cocoa powder, sugar, baking powder, baking soda and salt. Set aside.

In another bowl, whisk together the egg, milk, sour cream, melted butter and vanilla. Pour this mixture into the bowl of dry ingredients. Mix together (I use a rubber spatula) until a batter forms and all of the flour is incorporated. The batter should be on the thicker side.

Spoon the batter into your donut tray or muffin tin. Fill the cavities three-quarters full. Filling them all the way up will cause the donuts to be flat on the bottom. Bake for 9 to 12 minutes, or until you can insert a toothpick into the donut and it comes out clean.

While the donuts are baking, make the ganache. Place the chocolate chips in a heat-safe bowl. It helps if the chocolate is at room temperature when you start. Heat the heavy whipping cream in the microwave in a microwave-safe bowl for 2 minutes (or in a saucepan on the stove until simmering, meaning that bubbles are forming on the edges of the pan). Pour the hot cream over the chocolate. Let the ingredients sit for 1 minute, then whisk until a shiny chocolate sauce forms.

To frost the donuts, dip the round side of the donuts into the ganache, and for that special zing, I always add sprinkles on top.

GOLD STAR GLAZED DONUTS

Few things compare to the taste of fresh warm glazed donuts. I will warn you: Donut dough, or any yeasted dough for that matter, requires a bit of technical skill, but I know you can master this! Activating the yeast is the most crucial step. If the yeast dies/does not activate, you will have flat donuts! Little steps like kneading the dough require some additional attention to detail to ensure you have fluffy donuts.

YiELD: 1 dozen donuts
DiFFiCULTY: 🥄🥄

DONUTS

1¼ cups (300 ml) milk

1 package (2½ tsp; 9 g) active dry yeast

1 tbsp + ⅓ cup (81 g) granulated sugar, divided

½ cup (114 g; 1 stick) butter, melted

2 eggs

4¼ cups (530 g) all-purpose flour, plus more for rolling out the dough

1 tsp salt

Cooking spray

2 quarts (1.9 L) neutral oil (such as vegetable or canola), for frying

Place two sheets of wax or parchment paper over two baking sheets and set aside.

To make the donuts, pour the milk into a medium-sized microwave-safe bowl. Microwave for 30 seconds. If you don't have a microwave, heat the milk in a pot over low heat on the stove. The temperature of the milk is very important. We are going to add yeast, which is the ingredient that is key in this recipe. The yeast we are using is actually a living organism!! So, if your milk is too hot, it will kill the yeast, preventing your donuts from puffing up. I always use a candy thermometer to check the temperature of the milk, which should be 90°F (32°C). If you don't have a candy thermometer, dip your finger in the milk, and if it's warm but not hot enough to be uncomfortable, the milk is the right temperature. Sprinkle in the yeast and 1 tablespoon (15 g) of the sugar and stir for 10 seconds, then set the yeast bowl to the side for 10 minutes. After 10 minutes, your yeast should have developed foam on top. If not, your yeast was not properly activated and you should start this process again.

Pour the activated yeast into the bowl of a stand mixer with the melted butter, eggs and the remaining ⅓ cup (66 g) of sugar. Beat on medium speed, just until all the ingredients are incorporated, around 1 minute.

Add the flour and salt, and switch to the dough hook attachment on your mixer. If you don't have this attachment, you can mix the dough by hand with a wooden spoon.

When the flour and salt are mixed in and the dough comes together, you need to knead it for 8 minutes. Personally, I find it fun to knead the dough by hand. My technique is to press down the dough with the palm of my hand, then flip the dough over, and press down again, repeating these steps. Kneading by hand definitely gets tiring after a few minutes so instead, you can use the dough hook on the mixer. Set the mixer on low speed and forget about the dough for 8 to 10 minutes. You will knead the dough until it becomes beautifully smooth.

(continued)

GOLD STAR GLAZED DONUTS (CONT.)

After 8 minutes of kneading the dough, spray a large bowl with cooking spray, then drop the dough into the bowl. Cover the bowl with a layer of plastic wrap or a kitchen towel and let it rest for 1 hour, or until the dough has doubled in size. Letting the dough rest is called proofing the dough. If your dough does not get larger after letting it rest, this is a sign the yeast may not have activated.

GLAZE

2 tbsp (28 g) butter, melted

1½ cups (330 g) powdered sugar

1 tbsp (15 ml) evaporated milk

1 tsp vanilla extract

¼ tsp salt

After the dough has proofed, lightly "punch" or press down on the dough to release extra air, then lightly flour a work surface. Dump the dough onto the work surface and roll the dough out to a ½-inch (1.3-cm)-thick sheet. To cut out the donut shapes, you can use a round cookie cutter, but if you don't have one, you can use the rim of a drinking glass. To cut the hole in the middle, use your smallest cookie cutter (or use the cap of a water bottle). After cutting out your donuts, you will have plenty of dough scraps. Feel free to rework the excess dough into another ball and roll it out to create more donuts. Note that the more you work the dough, the tougher it will get, so work with it as little as you can.

Place the cut-out donuts on the prepared baking sheets, with a few inches (5 cm) of space between each donut, as the dough will expand again. Cover the baking sheets with a kitchen towel and let the dough rest for another 1 hour. It's best to let the dough rise in a warm area, like in your oven on the lowest setting, with the oven door open.

When the dough has risen, prepare the oil for frying. I have never owned a deep fryer, so I've always made fried food like donuts on the stove. Frying on the stove can be dangerous, as the hot oil can cause some serious burns. Always be super careful!

Pour the oil into a large pot or Dutch oven. Place the pot on the stove over medium heat. I usually use a thermometer to measure the temperature, as we want the oil to be 350°F (175°C), but if you don't have a thermometer, place the handle of a wooden spoon into the hot oil. If bubbles quickly form around the spoon handle, you're ready to fry your donuts.

Gently lift a donut from the baking sheet and, very carefully, lower it into the hot oil. Cook the donuts two at a time for 1 minute on each side, or until the donuts are golden brown. Remove the donuts from the oil and put onto a plate.

To make the glaze, mix the melted butter, powdered sugar, evaporated milk, vanilla and salt in a large bowl. Whisk together for 2 minutes, until all the ingredients are evenly combined. Dip the warm donuts into the glaze, using a spoon to coat the entire donut, and then place the donuts onto a cooling rack or serving tray. Let the donuts dry for 20 minutes, then enjoy.

For chocolate-frosted donuts, use this donut recipe with the chocolate ganache glaze recipe from the Chocolate Cake Donuts on page 157.

STRAWBERRY PiNK GLAZED DONUTS

I love the idea of bright-colored donuts that pack a punch of flavor. The aesthetic of the pink frosted donut is all over social media, TV shows, and even cartoons. Made with real strawberries, this strawberry frosting is a gourmet version of something you'd buy from the store.

YiELD: 1 dozen donuts
DiFFiCULTY: ✎✎

DONUTS

1 batch donut dough (from the Gold Star Glazed Donuts recipe on page 158)

STRAWBERRY GLAZE

2–3 strawberries

2 tbsp (28 g) melted butter

1½–2 cups (180–240 g) powdered sugar

½ tsp vanilla extract

2 drops red food coloring (optional)

Sprinkles (optional)

Follow the directions in the Gold Star Glazed Donuts recipe on page 158 to make and fry the donuts.

To make the strawberry glaze, add the strawberries to a food processor or blender. Blend on high speed until the strawberries are smooth, aka purée the strawberries. You should have 2 to 3 tablespoons (30 to 45 ml) of purée. Add the melted butter, 1½ cups (180 g) of the powdered sugar, the vanilla and red food coloring if you want the iconic pink color of strawberry glazed donuts and blend again until all the ingredients are evenly incorporated. For a thicker glaze, add more powdered sugar, 1 tablespoon (8 g) at a time, and mix again until you reach your desired consistency.

Pour the strawberry glaze into a shallow bowl and dip the warm donuts into the strawberry glaze. Finish with sprinkles (if using), and allow the donuts to cool for 10 minutes before enjoying.

JELLY-FiLLED DONUTS WiTH A TWiST

A standard jelly-filled donut is a tasty treat, but we're not about average here. Our ultimate jelly donuts take a different approach than the original, but in my opinion, this approach takes this donut to the next level. We are mixing a strawberry jam with fresh strawberries to fill the donuts, making the donuts extra fresh!

YiELD: 1 dozen donuts
DiFFiCULTY: 🥄🥄🥄

DONUTS

1 batch donuts (from the Gold Star Glazed Donuts recipe on page 158)

2 cups (240 g) powdered sugar

STRAWBERRY FILLING

1 quart (4 cups; 664 g) fresh strawberries

½ cup (100 g) granulated sugar

1 tbsp (15 ml) lemon juice

1 tbsp (8 g) cornstarch

1 tbsp (15 ml) water

Follow the directions in the Gold Star Glazed Donuts recipe on page 158 to make and fry the donuts, but do not cut a hole in the middle. Let them cool completely.

To make the strawberry filling, chop off the stems of the strawberries, then cut the strawberries into quarters. Place the strawberry quarters in a medium saucepan with the sugar and lemon juice over medium heat. Bring the mixture to a boil, 3 to 5 minutes, then reduce the heat to medium-low and cook for another 10 minutes, occasionally stirring.

Allow the strawberry mixture to cool for 10 minutes, then pour the cooled mixture into a blender, and blend for 1 to 2 minutes. When the strawberry mixture is smooth, pour it back into the saucepan.

In a small bowl, stir together the cornstarch and water, forming what is called a slurry. Mix the slurry into the strawberries in the saucepan. Cook for 3 minutes on medium heat until the sauce thickens.

Pour the powdered sugar into a shallow bowl or plate, then dip the cooled donuts into the powdered sugar, coating both top and bottom, as well as the sides of the donut.

Poke a hole through the side of the donuts (I use a piping tip or wooden skewer) and inject the donuts with the strawberry filling, using a piping bag or a ziptop bag with a bottom corner cut off. These donuts are over-the-top, delicious and fun to make.

MAPLE-BACON DONUTS

Nothing pops out quite like a maple-bacon donut. I get hungry just thinking about the maple-bacon combo, which is the ultimate breakfast flavor. Plus, people eat donuts for breakfast and bacon for breakfast, so we're basically making the best breakfast food of all time. The salty and sweet blend of the flavors creates a donut like no other.

YiELD: 1 dozen donuts

DiFFiCULTY: ✎ ✎ ✎

DONUTS
1 batch donuts (from the Gold Star Glazed Donuts recipe on page 158)

CANDIED BACON
12 slices uncooked bacon

2 tbsp (28 g) brown sugar

MAPLE GLAZE
3½ tbsp (49 g) butter, melted

½ cup (120 ml) pure maple syrup

1¾ cups (210 g) powdered sugar

¼ tsp maple extract

½ tsp vanilla extract

¼ tsp salt

Follow the directions in the Gold Star Glazed Donuts recipe on page 158 to make and fry the donuts. Let them cool completely.

To make the bacon, preheat the oven to 350°F (175°C) and line a large baking sheet with parchment paper.

Until a year ago, I always cooked my bacon in a pan on the stove. That was until I learned the magic of oven-cooked bacon! It is so much less effort to pop a tray of bacon in the oven.

Place the bacon on the parchment-lined baking sheet. It's OK if the bacon slices slightly overlap, as they will shrink. Sprinkle the brown sugar over the bacon, then bake for 18 to 20 minutes, until the bacon has reached prime crispiness. Remove the bacon from the oven, pat the slices dry with a paper towel, then, when it has cooled slightly, using your hands or a knife, break up the bacon slices into smaller pieces.

While the bacon is baking, make the maple glaze. Pour the melted butter and maple syrup into a large bowl and whisk until combined. Add the powdered sugar, maple extract, vanilla extract and salt. Whisk until the batter is smooth and no lumps of sugar remain, 1 to 2 minutes.

To assemble the donuts, dip a donut into the maple glaze then place on a serving tray. Sprinkle with the pieces of bacon and serve this fun twist on a traditional donut.

RED VELVET CAKE DONUTS

A fun spin on the traditional cake donut, the red velvet donut is the perfect combination of a kitchen classic with a little kick of creativity. The fluffy red velvet donuts paired with the tangy cream cheese icing is definitely a donut to remember.

YIELD: 12 donuts
DIFFICULTY: 🥄

RED VELVET DONUTS

Cooking spray

¾ cup (150 g) granulated sugar

2 tsp (4 g) cocoa powder

¼ tsp salt

½ tsp baking soda

1¼ cups (155 g) all-purpose flour

½ cup (120 ml) buttermilk (see Note)

½ cup (120 ml) vegetable oil

1 tsp vanilla extract

½ tsp distilled white vinegar

1 tbsp (15 ml) red food coloring

CREAM CHEESE ICING

3 oz (85 g) cream cheese, softened

2 tbsp (28 g) butter, at room temperature

2 cups (240 g) powdered sugar

½ tsp vanilla extract

2–3 tbsp (30–45 ml) milk

Preheat the oven to 350°F (175°C) and generously spray a donut tray with cooking spray, or if you don't have a donut tray, spray a muffin tin with cooking spray.

In a large bowl, whisk together the sugar, cocoa powder, salt, baking soda and flour. Set aside.

In a medium bowl, whisk together the buttermilk, vegetable oil, vanilla, vinegar and red food coloring.

Pour the wet ingredients into the flour mixture and use a wooden spoon to mix the ingredients into a batter.

Spoon the batter into your donut tray or muffin tin. Fill the cavities three-quarters full. Filling them all the way up will cause the donuts to be flat on the bottom. Bake for 9 to 12 minutes, or until you can insert a toothpick into the donut and it comes out clean.

While the donuts are baking, make the cream cheese icing. In a medium bowl, mix together the cream cheese and butter. When well combined, stir in the powdered sugar, vanilla and milk. Mix until an icing forms.

To frost the donuts, my favorite way of decorating is to fill a piping bag with frosting then snip the bottom off. If you don't have a piping bag, fill a ziptop bag with the frosting and snip one of the bottom corners off. Squeeze the frosting over the donuts, drizzling it on top.

NOTE: See page 11 to learn how to make your own buttermilk.

ACKNOWLEDGMENTS

I would be remiss if I didn't thank my parents. They have done everything they can to support me as a chef and a person and I am eternally grateful for the sacrifices they have made for me, which have brought me to where I am today. Whether it be late-night kitchen cleanups or hopping on a plane to Los Angeles for an indefinite amount of time, they are the best parents I could ask for.

Thank you to Veronica and Jon Jon, my siblings, for all that you've done for me growing up. Veronica always helps me with the dishes, so big shoutout to her. I love you guys so much.

Thank you to my high school English teachers, who have taught me so much about writing, especially Ms. Denizé, Dr. Licato, Dr. Hoyrd and Mr. Schultz. Thank you to my history teachers, Mr. Campbell and Mr. Mills, for encouraging me to make writing interesting and hook the reader.

I am so grateful for Page Street Publishing, specifically Marissa and Meg. Marissa guided me through the entire book-writing process, which seemed super daunting at first. She put a lot of faith in me and I've had such a great experience working on this book.

Thank you to Tom McGovern for shooting the beautiful photography. I learned so much from the entire photography process and working with him.

To Bibi, thank you so much for fostering a love of cooking in me from a young age, even though there are still some recipes you won't share. . . .

To Grammy and Gramps, I owe so much of my love of baking to you both. You have always been so supportive of my baking endeavors, and it is always such a pleasure to bake for you both.

Thank you to my foodie friends who I've met on TikTok—you all inspire me every day.

Thank you to Diana Jeffra, whose expertise in food styling helped make these photos fantastic.

Thank you to Simone Payment for her amazing editing skills.

ABOUT THE AUTHOR

Matthew Merril has lived his entire life (a whopping 16 years!) in the Washington, DC, area, where he has cultivated a passion for all things culinary. Inspired by the magic of Christmas cookies made annually, Matthew was fascinated by the concept of baking, fueling his early-childhood obsession with food television. After sending an email from his mom's computer, Matthew was given the opportunity of a lifetime to compete on Food Network's *Kids Baking Championship* at the age of 10. After making it all the way to the finals, Matthew made appearances on a handful of other shows, including *Chopped Junior*, *Guy's Grocery Games*, *Holiday Baking Championship* and more. Following his work on Food Network, Merril began high school, as well as his TikTok page, finding time during the 2020 COVID-19 pandemic to launch his first videos. Matthew gained more than 2 million followers in just one year with his creative and informative cooking demos. As a result, Matthew has been able to work with incredible brands and even write his very own cookbook.

iNDEX